See You In Kirk Yetholm

Tales from the Pennine Way

Andrew Bowden

Text and photographs
©2015 Andrew Paul Bowden
All rights reserved

The right of Andrew Bowden to be identified as the Author of the work has been asserted by him in accordance with the Copyright, Designs and Patents Act 1998.

First published, 2015

ISBN 1511673575
ISBN-13 978-1511673570

To the fells...

Contents

Introduction..9
Part 1...15
  Edale to Crowden..................................17
  Crowden to Diggle.................................29
  Diggle to Hebden Bridge.......................39
  Hebden Bridge to Ponden.....................51
  Ponden to Earby....................................59
  Earby to Gargrave.................................69
Part 2...75
  Gargrave to Malham..............................77
  Malham to Horton-in-Ribblesdale...................85
Part 3...95
  Horton-in-Ribblesdale to Hawes.......................97
  Hawes to Tan Hill Inn...........................107
  Tan Hill Inn to Middleton-in-Teesdale............121
  Middleton-in-Teesdale to Dufton.....................133
Part 4...143
  Dufton to Garrigill.............................145
  Garrigill to Slaggyford.........................157
  Slaggyford to Greenhead......................171
  Greenhead to Once Brewed..................181
  Once Brewed to Bellingham.................193
  Bellingham to Byrness........................207
  Stuck in Byrness.................................219
Part 5...227
  Byrness to Windy Gyle.......................229
  Windy Gyle to Kirk Yetholm...............243

Epilogue	257
About The Author	263
Planning your own Pennine Way walk	265
Discover other books by Andrew Bowden	278
Connect with Andrew Bowden	279

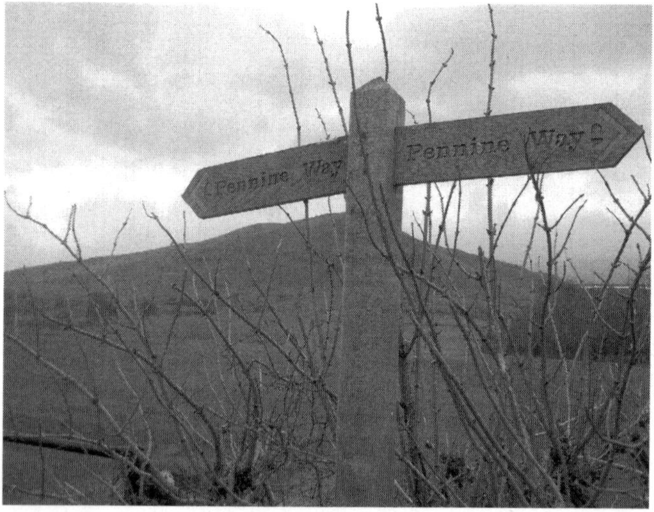

Pennine Way
Pennine Way

Introduction

The seeds may be small, but if they're planted in just the right spot and given just the right conditions, then it's quite possible that a mighty tree may grow. Or, to put it in a slightly less prosaic way, everything has to start somewhere.

And for me, my love of walking, which has seen me walk thousands of miles across the United Kingdom of Great Britain and Northern Ireland, was planted, nourished and grew, on the Pennine Way.

For those that don't know it, the Pennine Way is the grandfather of walking trails in the UK. Its creation was first suggested by journalist and rambler Tom Stephenson in an article for the Daily Herald newspaper, published in 1935. He was inspired by the two thousand mile long Appalachian Trail that was being created in the United States of America at the time. If something like that could be done in the US, why not in Britain?

It took thirty years for the dream to become reality, but on Saturday, 24 April 1965 the Pennine Way was officially opened for business. Stretching across the Pennine hills, the backbone of the country, the trail set off from Edale in Derbyshire, slowly but surely making its way through the north of England before, close to the end, hopping over the border into Scotland and finishing in the small town of Kirk Yetholm. On its way, it passes through the UK's first National Park – the Peak District – and makes its way through the Yorkshire Dales and Northumberland National Parks as well. For good measure it visits Hadrian's Wall, and even treats the Cheviot hills as "honorary" Pennines.

The Pennine Way was the very first National Trail, created by the state, and protected by law. It would be the first of many. The second, the Cleveland Way, followed four years later, and now there are fifteen National Trails in England and Wales, and four official "Long Distance Routes" in Scotland. And that's before we've counted the hundreds of other walking routes – created by all manner of local councils, walking organisations and even individuals – that spread across the country. Walks based on geographical features like rivers and hill ranges, more arbitrary routes around county borders, or trails simply created by someone who wanted to create a bloomin' good walk. But the Pennine Way is the grandfather of them all. The first. The oldest.

It's no easy trail either. It's one of England's more challenging trails, going over remote moorland, passing through quiet villages, and providing the walker with ever so many chances to put their foot, and perhaps their whole body, into plenty of peat bog.

Not that I really knew any of this when I first set foot on the trail. Indeed, despite the fact that I grew up less than ten miles away from one section,

I knew next to nothing about it. But then, I was never a massively keen walker as a child. My parents would take us off on Sundays for an afternoon wander on the nearby hill which dominated the town we lived in, and would occasionally decide to broaden their walking horizons by heading off around a reservoir or some local moorland. However by my teens, dimly muttering the word "homework" was all that was needed to avoid such trips.

And so it remained, until a year or so after leaving university. I'd moved to London with my partner Catherine.

Catherine liked walking. She'd even completed a National Trail – the Pembrokeshire Coast Path – aged nine. And she wasn't going to let living in the largest city in the country prevent her from heading out.

"Let's go for a walk!" she'd say, before taking us off to wander down some litter strewn canal towpath in west London, or a muddy park near a golf course. Slowly but surely, the walks got a little more adventurous, heading out for day walks across the south of England.

And then one day, she came out with it.

"Let's go away for a weekend. We can go walking!"

Her plan was simple. We'd catch the train to Yorkshire and walk a bit of the Pennine Way from Gargrave to Horton-in-Ribblesdale. This would take two days, and then we'd spend a third day checking out two of the Dales's three peaks:

Ingleborough and Whernside (the third peak, Pen-y-ghent, forming part of our Pennine Way walk.) Oh, and there'd be country inns with fantastic Yorkshire beer on the bar, she added knowing full well how to hook me in.

It rained heavily on our first morning and we spent lunch huddling next to a roaring fire in a Malham pub trying to dry out. It may have been the end of March but some fields were still deeply covered in snow. We'd even passed a dead sheep.

The next day we climbed Pen-y-ghent in the mist, and the day after headed out for our circular walk, up Ingleborough and Whernside in absolutely fantastic weather. It was glorious; beautiful beyond belief.

The seeds had been sown. The ground was good, and the conditions were just right. I was hooked. The scenery helped, but there was also something about walking from one place to another that just worked for me. Exploring new places, seeing new sights. As we sat in the Crown Inn in Horton-in-Ribblesdale on our final evening, I muttered some immortal words.

"I think I could do some more of this Pennine Way thing."

And that was that. Seven months later we were back in Horton to do another stretch up to Dufton. The next spring we caught the train to Edale so we could do the start of the walk. And so it went on until three years later, we found ourselves at Kirk Yetholm, supping a pint in celebration at the Border Inn having finally completed the whole thing.

It wasn't the first walking trail that I completed. That honour went to the South Downs Way. And it certainly wouldn't be the last. But the Pennine Way was the first I started actually walking. Just as the birth of the Pennine Way spawned a number of new walking trails, so the Pennine Way set me off walking many more trails.

Part 1

Edale to Gargrave
Third trip walking the Pennine Way

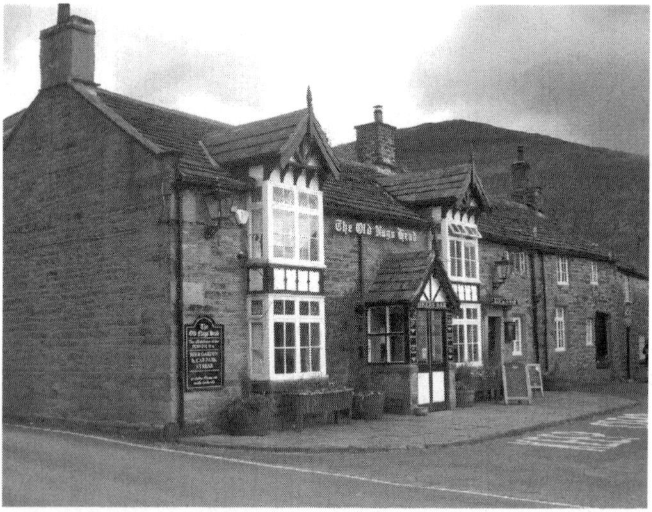
The Old Nags Head

Edale to Crowden

The Old Nags Head, Edale. The official start of the Pennine Way. Or "official start of the Pennine Wa" as the sign outside the pub actually said on the day I stood next to it, grinning like a loon for the statutory "I'm setting off for a walk!" photograph.

And I was setting off for a walk. Although, in some respects I also wasn't. For whilst I may have been in Edale at the very start of the Pennine Way, I had also walked nearly a third of the trail already.

This was something that the part of me that has a very neat and ordered mind, was struggling with. You start at the beginning, go through the middle and then get to the end. It's clear, logical and sensible. It's as it should be. If you sat down today with the aim of planning your own walk on the Pennine Way, that's no doubt how you'd tackle it.

And that is, of course, the problem. In the beginning we'd never intended to walk the whole of the trail. The decision to do so came later. And that meant that our first footsteps on the Pennine Way were roughly a third of the way in. And then when we returned for a second go, we simply continued from where we left off. All of which meant there was a gaping hole to fill. The start. Which was why I was now stood at the start of the Pennine Way a year after I'd first started walking it.

It was all very confusing. Probably best not to think about it really, and instead contemplate on the fact that the sun was shining; the going looked good. We didn't quite have 268 miles to do, but it was certainly time to get walking.

* * *

For a trail that goes over wild moorland, bogs and many hills, and that has a reputation of being a tough beast to tackle, the Pennine Way starts rather sedately. It creeps gently along fields, around the base of a hill, and along a rather wide and easy going path. It's a nice path with some lovely views to admire – the Peak District is a fantastic place, after all – however the finest, looking down the Edale Valley, did require us to stop and turn round in order to enjoy it. Either that or we'd have to walk backwards. And that has it owns risks.

If you didn't know anything about the Pennine Way, then walking those first couple of miles would very quickly lull you into a false sense of security. Ah this is the life, you'd think to yourself. Nice easy stroll with some lovely views. How relaxing. And then you'd arrive at Jacob's Ladder and realise that, confound it, this was a trail that was going to make you work after all.

The ladder is not one path but two, and it's all named after an 18th century farmer called Jacob Marshall, who was the person who built both paths. The two are different lengths. The longer one slowly but surely zig-zags up the hill at a gentler gradient; the kind that would be taken by a pack horse. The shorter of the two is steeper; a path that would allow the person leading the horses to quickly get to the top of the hill, sit down and have a rest whilst his charges slowly meandered up the other path.

When all is said and done, Jacob's Ladder isn't a massive climb, however it was a sign of things to come. A hint that the Pennine Way isn't a mild wander through pleasant valleys. Sometimes it gets difficult. There are hills to climb you know.

Naturally we entered into the spirit of the ladder. By taking the longer way up. Well if it's good enough for the horses...

* * *

For some reason, the Pennine Way doesn't pass by Edale Cross. Given it's a local landmark, this seems a rather strange and curious omission. For that reason alone scores of Pennine Way walkers take the short detour to pay homage to this simple stone.

No one really knows how old the cross is, or exactly why it was put there. It's believed by some to be medieval, and quite possibly erected as an administrative boundary marker by the Abbots of the Basingwerk Abbey who, despite being based in Wales, owned and managed a vast estate in the Peak District.

What is known is that over the years, the cross fell down, and spent many years on the ground until 1810 when five local farmers re-erected it. When they did, they left their own mark on it (or vandalised the cross – take your pick) by carving their initials into the stone. We duly paid our respects to whoever had put the cross there in the first place, and then headed to another landmark; one which firmly has a place in walking history. Kinder Scout.

Kinder is a special enough place as it is. The highest point in the Peak District, with views of Snowdonia on a good day. Its peat groughs, large stones and heather can sometimes make you feel like you're walking in another world. However Kinder's more than just a fantastic piece of landscape; it's part of walking history.

As with much of the countryside at the time, the hills of the Peak District were firmly off limit to most people; access restricted to the landowners, and enforced by their staff. Those living in the crowded and polluted towns nearby could only look on and stare. Their desire to get out into the clean air and enjoy the countryside was denied.

Located slap bang between Sheffield and Manchester, it's no real surprise that the Peak District was a prime target for those campaigning to open up access to the countryside and in 1932, Kinder Scout became a focal point of the campaign, as ramblers headed towards it from the nearby village of Hayfield, in order to invade the fell en masse.

Naturally the attempt to claim Kinder for the people didn't go unchallenged. Gamekeepers, employed by the landowners, tried to restrict access and there were many violent scuffles. Their efforts were in vain. Several hundred walkers from Manchester reached the top of Kinder, where they met up with a party of 30 of Sheffield's residents who had headed up from Jacob's Ladder.

The story of working people challenging the order of the day naturally attracted press attention and the walkers were joined by a journalist from the Manchester Guardian newspaper. The resulting newspaper report helped raise awareness of the campaign, and helped bolster the cause even further. In the aftermath of the trespass five ramblers were arrested, and some were given jail sentences for their part in the scuffles. It was a decision that fuelled the campaign even further, and turned the tide in favour of reform, to the disgust of many of the landowners.

It wasn't an overnight victory. Indeed, it took nearly twenty years in the end – a certain World War II helping to stall things – but in 1949 the National Parks and Access to the Countryside Act was passed, which laid the foundation for creating National Parks, and access to open land. Two years later, the Peak District National Park formally opened for business. Other national parks followed, and then, of course, in 1965 came the Pennine Way. Although it was as recently as 2000 that the Countryside and Rights of Way Act finally opened up swathes of "access land" in England and Wales where the public could roam anywhere, freely.

With so much time passed by, it's easy to take it all for granted. But only a couple of generations earlier, we wouldn't have been able to do what we were doing right now. There are some who believe that the Kinder Trespass set back the whole right to roam campaign; that it invoked a fight back from the landowners and, therefore, delayed the inevitable. We'll never know for sure. But standing on Kinder Scout, looking down on the towns and villages nearby, many a quiet thanks has been given to all those who kept up the fight for so long.

* * *

Stone slabs lead their way over Mill Hill, over Featherbed Moss and onto Bleaklow. The slabs are a familiar sight for anyone walking the Pennine Way; introduced by the authorities to solve the problems of erosion caused by decades of walkers traversing the soft, peaty land. Several times the flagged path had taken a slightly different course to the original route, but here and there the flags had been laid on the original path, which would give an inclination why the authorities had taken the action they did. On a couple of such sections, the walls of peat on either side of the path were almost as tall as I was; the peat having eroded so much under thousands of pairs of walking boots.

It was a sign of how much the land had changed since walkers had arrived on the hills, and a clear demonstration of the conflicting demands of access to the countryside, and the need to conserve it for the future.

The path crossed the A57 road, linking Manchester with Sheffield, and which – funnily enough – passes right through the town I grew up in. After that, it heads onto Bleaklow, which didn't seem especially bleak on this sunny day, and at a height of 633m above sea level, nor was it particularly low. Bleaklow famously contains the wreckage of an old US Air Force bomber that crashed on the hillside in 1948, killing all 13 crew members on board. The remains of the plane can be found on the hillside to this day, and the site is so well known that Pennine Way walkers regularly divert off route to pay their respects.

Those that know about it anyway. Our guidebook had decided that it wasn't worthy of a mention.

The guidebook did however deem another famous landmark important enough to mention. Sitting a short way from Bleaklow's summit, the Wain Stones are a pair of weathered stones which, from the right angle, gave the impression of an old man and woman puckering up for a kiss. It's a famous photo opportunity with walkers who strive to get the shot and angle just right. Naturally a few botch it, managing to take the picture from completely the wrong side, or getting the angle slightly wrong. And of course, I was one of those who fitted firmly in the latter category.

What can I say? This was all new to me and, just like the bomber crash site, I'd never heard of the Wain Stones and didn't know what was 'wain' about them either. I took the best guess I could, and ended up with a photograph of two rocks sticking together. Would it really have hurt the guide book author to put in a suitably representative snap that novices like me could use as a guideline? I mean, our tome had several pages all about cotton grass and heather. A quick photo of some stones would be easy to fit in, or so you'd think.

My photographic errors were then followed by a cock-up of epic proportions. The mistake however, wasn't mine. Navigation was firmly the responsibility of Catherine, my accomplice in crime for the entire Pennine Way journey, who had taken charge of the proceedings from day one after confidently declaring she could easily use a map and a compass. As my own skills had been a tad rusty, I'd naturally agreed, thus freeing me of any responsibility for the massive error we were about to make.

From the Wain Stones, all we needed to do was head north a short way then follow the clear path off to the west. Simple. Instead, we managed to head east, walking in completely the wrong direction and rather precariously down a narrow clough alongside a stream.

We were half way down to the valley floor when the mistake was finally discovered. Too far along to turn back certainly. It was to be a costly detour; one which would see us four miles away from where we should have been. Which, given we were supposed to be meeting someone there in a car, was a bit of an issue.

With limited accommodation in Crowden – basically a camp-site and a (now closed) youth hostel – we'd arranged something else. One of the benefits of growing up in the area was that we just happened to have handy and convenient supply of relatives to stay with, based just a few miles down the road. We'd arranged to stay with Catherine's parents who were due to pick us up at the car park at Crowden. We'd called them at home earlier with a rough ETA, but somehow we had to redirect their efforts. Thankfully the invention of the mobile phone had helped us in this respect. But Catherine's parents had not exactly adapted well to the mobile era. Whilst they did have one, they had a habit of leaving it uncharged in their drawer in their dining room at home.

My feet were aching enough as it was; at sixteen mile long, Edale to Crowden's not a particularly short first day, and the thought of having to do another four and hope that there would still be someone there to meet us, was filling me with dread. But thankfully we were in luck. After half an hour of trying to get a mobile signal, we finally got through. Their phone had made it out with them after all, and fifteen minutes later we were being whisked away by motor vehicle.

After a day in the quiet hills of the Peaks, we were suddenly being transported to the bright lights of the suburbs of Manchester. A part of it felt so wrong to be leaving the quiet hills for a town with several supermarkets, curry houses and a grand Victorian town hall. On the other hand, we were going somewhere with free food, drink and lodgings. And who really would argue with that?

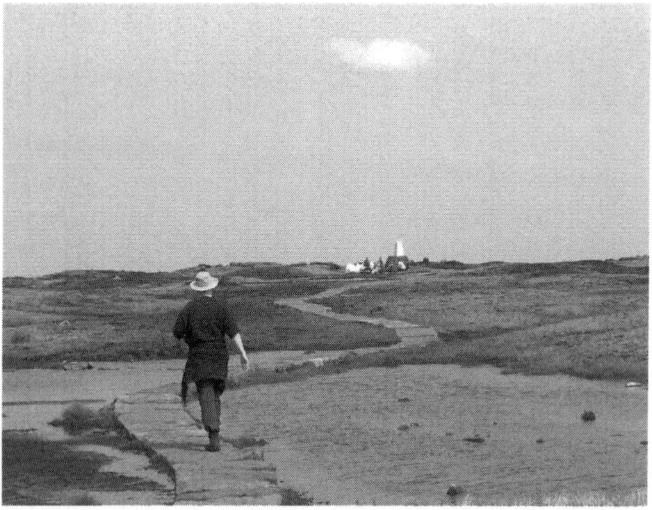

Crowden to Diggle

Put yourself in this scene. In a few months' time you will be travelling several thousand miles by plane to Nepal. After a couple of days in Kathmandu checking out the local sights, you'll leave the city to set off on a walk. For several days you'll walk towards Everest Basecamp, staying at little villages every evening. It'll be a good, well made path, but it will be one which will take you steadily up hill.

In your planning you note that you need to do some preparation for the trip; get yourself up to the level of fitness that will be demanded for such a trip. You've done a lot of walking over the years and the hills are no stranger to you. But there's one thing you're a little worried about. The plan will see you carrying all your belongings in a rucksack. It's been a while since you've carried such a heavy load on your back. You begin to think that you probably should get some practice in before you go out there.

Meanwhile, your daughter's been on the phone. She tells you that she'll be walking a section of the Pennine Way this May with her partner. And that gives you an idea. Your daughter always carries her own rucksack with her when she's doing walking trips. So why don't you offer to join them on the second day on the Pennine Way? You could carry their rucksacks for them. It will be good practice.

And so it was that the next morning we got out of the car at Crowden and set off along the Pennine Way, having been relieved of our rucksacks, which were now being ably carried by our two sherpas, also known as Catherine's parents, Mike and Julie. Their plan was to walk with us for the five or so miles to Black Hill, gaining invaluable insight into carrying several kilograms of weight on their backs. Once they got there they'd return our luggage, bid us farewell and head back to their car, parked up back at Crowden.

Well, I wasn't going to argue. I always carry my own stuff when out hiking rather than paying someone to transport it for me. But it's still always nice when you don't have to carry anything at all. Instead of grunting as you struggle to slowly climb that steep hill, you can skip up it in a sprightly fashion. Or, at least, walk a bit faster. And the difference that a pack (or lack of) can make to walking speed was soon revealed by the way we suddenly found ourselves travelling much faster than our luggage.

The rucksacks weren't entirely to blame. Mike was also weighed down by his substantially sized digital camera. Naturally this was not one of those "point and fire" devices, but one which required copious twiddling knobs and adjusting of focus to get the perfect shot in the way that camera experts do. In the time it took him just to assemble his giant photographic apparatus, focus in on the subject and take a picture, I'd usually be able to whip out my distinctly more compact camera, hit the shutter button, put it away and be half a mile away. Not that it put him off. Mighty rocks, tufts of browning grass, large clumps of heather; all were fair game for Mike's giant lens. And the Pennine Way offered them in abundance. Attractive streams were a firm favourite for the camera lens, as they crept slowly down the hillside, flowing beautifully through rocks, just as they must have done for centuries. The mighty camera was frequently assembled and disassembled, as shot after shot was taken, and another few metres walked. Watching, I wasn't quite sure I'd have the patience.

Still, we made it along, and silently, and without fanfare, we reached the top of Dun Hill where a milestone was waiting for us. Not a physical one, but one none-the-less. For the summit marked a boundary. The point when we'd leave Derbyshire and enter our second county, the county of Yorkshire.

* * *

"Black Hill's a morass!" is a common accusation of the place. It does have rather a reputation for wet peat, making going difficult for walkers. Massive pools of peaty water can swallow a boot in seconds, which can be rather off-putting. On the other hand, they can create a dramatic scene for a photograph, so it really does depend on your point of view. Not for nothing do some walkers avoid the whole place, giving it all up as a bad lot.

These days though, Black Hill's reputation is rather unfair and those dank, dark pools aren't anything to worry about. At least, as long as you stay on the paved paths that criss-cross the hill. Put a foot wrong though and you may never be seen again.

Looking at those pools of dark water from the safety of a stone paving flag however, does give you an impression of what the Pennine Way must have been before the paving was put in. How people coped with Black Hill before, I didn't know. I could only imagine what this route must have been like for much of its life. Maybe I would have reached Black Hill's top, taken one look at it, and headed off to the bright lights of the nearby town of Glossop instead, never to set foot on the Pennine Way again. There are some who cry that the paving slabs have ruined the character of the Pennine Way; that this is what the countryside is really like, and that's what must be embraced; that the Pennine Way now is little different to an urban street, but if you'd asked most of the people on Black Hill that day whether the flags should be ripped up, I doubt most would have taken you up on it.

Besides, it's not like the entire hill has been tarmacked over. There are still some side trails which head off in random directions if you wish to dice with danger and peat bog. One of those was about to be followed by Catherine's parents as they headed back to their car. Rucksacks were exchanged; best wishes and hugs given. And then they were off, bouncing over the hillside with just a large camera bag between them.

And how did it help them on their Nepal trip go, you ask? Did the practice carrying all our luggage help them on their trip? Well, they did walk a day carrying their own stuff. And then they did what most visitors do when walking in Nepal. They employed a local sherpa to carry it all for them. By all accounts, in one deft move, the sherpa had lashed the two rucksacks together with rope, and started carrying them both on his back with relative ease, all whilst walking around the trail in flip flops.

* * *

According to popular wisdom, Snoopy's Snack Van on the A635 near Wessenden Head is a purveyor of the largest bacon butties known to man. Whether this is an exaggeration or really is reality, I can't tell you. I haven't conducted extensive research on the matter. Didn't even try one of Snoopy's apparent finest. We passed by the white van not feeling particularly hungry. And besides, Catherine is vegetarian. But whatever the size of the food served at this slightly innocuous white van in a remote spot, the number of cars parked up in the lay-by next to it suggested Snoopy was doing a roaring trade.

Snoopy's is just the latest of a long line of

purveyors of refreshment on this wild moorland. Up until the 1950s, the role was fulfilled by the Isle of Skye Hotel, although quite how it got that name is another question entirely. The place was hardly close to any Scottish isle after all. However anyone wanting a pint now will be out of luck as the pub's fate was sealed during the planning stages of the nearby Digley reservoir.

A compulsory purchase order was slapped on the property due to fears of the pub polluting the water that fed into the reservoir. A local battle ensued in an attempt to save it, but it was to no avail and the building was demolished afterwards. Well that's the story according to most sources. The other one occasionally proffered is that it was demolished after a fire; local fire engines being unable to reach it due to heavy snows having blocked the roads.

Whichever is accurate, there's now little on the ground to mark the fact that there was a pub there at all; the only reminder being that the section of the A635 continues to be locally known as Isle of Skye Road to this day.

The Pennine Way doesn't pass the site of all this controversy; Digley reservoir is actually a couple of miles away. However, there's still plenty of water based action for the walker in the area, as the trail goes past Black Moss, Wessenden, Swellands and Redbrook reservoirs; all of which sit on the moorland quietly collecting and storing water for when it's needed.

With its high rainfall, the Pennine hills naturally

caught the eyes of the authorities of the nearby conurbations of Manchester and Sheffield. The various towns and cities needed a source of good, clean water for the ever growing population to drink, as well as supplying factories and businesses. It was for the people of Huddersfield that Digley and Wessenden were built, whilst Swellands and Redbrook found other uses, namely to supply the Huddersfield Narrow Canal.

The Pennine Way made its way casually along as many of these reservoirs as it could muster, before depositing us quietly on the road at Standedge. The end of our walking day had been reached, and there was just one more task to do; head downhill to our B&B.

There are two options for accommodation for those arriving at Standedge. Turn right for the Yorkshire village of Marsden, or turn left for Greater Manchester and Diggle. The latter is slightly smaller but also just that bit nearer, which seemed a good enough reason to go with it. Now we just had to walk the mile and a half required to get there. But which route to follow? Take the simple but dull route down the main road, or follow the more sedate stylings of the Oldham Way – a forty mile stroll round the local Metropolitan Borough of Oldham – through fields of mud and sheep.

Naturally we opted for the option with the least tarmac and soon found ourselves covered in mud and sheep poo, stood in quiet, cosy street wandering around in circles wondering which of the many stone cottages housed the B&B that we'd been told was very easy to spot when you got there. For ten minutes we wandered around the place, getting increasingly more confused and frustrated at our ability to find the place. In the end we had to resort to using the telephone, where it turned out after a chat with a confused landlady, that we were in completely the wrong part of Diggle all along.

Thankfully, the village pub was far easier to find. Being a Friday night the place was bustling with locals happily chatting as they devoured huge platefuls of food. We joined them, relaxing with a couple of pints and resting our weary feet; those paving slabs being just a bit tough on the feet. Still, if it meant we didn't end up up to our waists in peat bog, that was something I was more than happy to put up with.

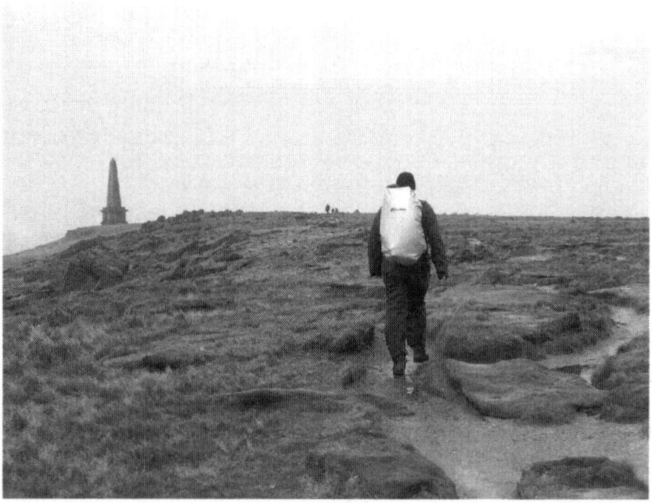

Diggle to Hebden Bridge

On the crowded bookshelves in my house can be found my favourite books about walking. In the hilarious "Pennine Walkies", Mark Wallington recounts his tales of walking the Pennine Way (funnily enough) with his dog Boogie. The excuse given for the endeavour was that someone who was middle-aged needed an adventure; something exciting that would be preferential to sitting in front of the television set all day. Apparently that someone was Boogie. So over the course of a couple of weeks, the aforementioned canine, ably accompanied by his owner, headed north from their home near Edale, with Mark carrying everything they needed in his rucksack, complete with several kilograms of complete dog food.

But more remarkable than the excuse given for walking the trail, or the fact that Wallington did the whole thing carrying food for two, is that the fact that the intrepid duo walked the whole thing in great weather.

Weather is so important when walking. There's nothing worse than spending day after day traipsing around in heavy rain; water seeping into your boots. No, good weather is what you want. Not *too* good of course, for you don't want to be walking when it's too hot. But somewhere in between. A bit of sun, a cool breeze and, most importantly, dry, very dry indeed.

Wallington had the dream scenario, and no mistake. We were to be less fortunate. After two days of near perfect weather, we were leaving Diggle prepared for the inevitable. Waterproofs and rucksack covers had been donned, and we set out of the door onto moorland hid under low level cloud, which was doing its best to make everywhere wet.

I've never been a fan of walking of the rain. I know there's that old Scandinavian saying that "there's no such thing as bad weather, just bad clothing" (although to be fair, I was wearing a particularly shoddy pair of waterproofs) but no matter how good your walking boots are, walking on slippery rocks is rarely fun. And that's just what the Pennine Way had in store for us over the course of the day.

But that was ahead of us. First we had to get there, making our way through the gloomy conditions; the Windy Hill transmitter ahead providing a good landmark to aim towards should we ever mislay the path. Which wasn't likely as the cloud levels weren't that low, but still, it's nice to know you're heading in the right direction.

And that direction was Yorkshire. Or West Yorkshire to be precise; a boundary marked with Greater Manchester by an extremely battered and worn sign at the side of the road. A sign emblazoned with a rose. It was probably supposed to be a white rose, but time had paid its toll and after years of standing on a desolate windswept piece of moorland the white rose of Yorkshire was definitely now more of a dull, murky grey.

A more modern sign – in far better condition – stood nearby, welcoming walkers and drivers not to Yorkshire – West or otherwise – but instead to Calderdale. What? No county pride up here, I hear you say? Well, no, for generally the only people who ever erect signs welcoming you to a county are a county council, and West Yorkshire doesn't have one. West Yorkshire County Council ceased to be in 1986, abolished by the Thatcher government who decided that the last thing large metropolitan areas such as West Yorkshire, the West Midlands and Greater London needed was an over-arching body to coordinate and manage services. The council's demise also meant there was no one love and care for that West Yorkshire sign.

Over on the other side of the boundary, an old white stone marker declared that people were now entering Lancashire, and specifically the area of the "Milnrow Local Board", which has been defunct even longer than West Yorkshire County Council. The Local Board was axed in 1894, replaced by Milnrow Urban District Council, which itself reigned until 1974 when the whole caboodle was shifted out of Lancashire and into the shiny new Metropolitan Borough of Rochdale, part of the new Greater Manchester county – whose county council was similarly culled by a certain axe-wielding female Prime Minister.

It is here that I risk the wrath of some of my readers. "Milnrow has always been Lancashire" they'll say. "That Greater Manchester thing is a myth. An abomination. A travesty. Lancashire we were, Lancashire we are, and Lancashire we always will be."

There will similar tales from people in Saddleworth, the Ridings of Yorkshire and more. That these modern counties are fake; that they are nothing, and certainly not a patch on their right and PROPER county affiliation.

It's an attitude I personally struggle to understand, for what, when all is said and done, is a county? Merely an arbitrary division of land, created for the purposes of administration, law making and revenue generation from the levy of taxes. The fact that some counties have existed for centuries, and some only for decades doesn't alter the only reason they actually exist at all. There is nothing intrinsically sacred about any county, new or old. It's just a plot of land which someone at some point has declared "Yes, this is it. Everything on the inside of this squiggle on this map, is the place and everything outside isn't."

And the fact is that in 1974, that definer of arbitrary lines decided that Milnrow was no more to be governed from Lancaster, reversing a decision made by another definer of arbitrary lines centuries earlier. These days it's a decision made by civil servants based on local demographics. Back then it was because some king had given a patch of land to one of their mates. No, the truth is that there's nothing especially sacred about the historic counties Lancashire, Yorkshire or any of their colleagues. They're just older and, frankly, a lot more arbitrary.

Having said all that – and no doubt having now caused some readers to abandon reading in utter disgust, and – there's a certain irony that in 2014 a new body was created. The West Yorkshire Combined Authority. And maybe if we give them a few years, they'll put a new sign up.

* * *

Even a quarter of a mile away, the road noise from the M62 was more than noticeable. Six lane motorways aren't the quietest of things. Hundreds of thousands of cars, lorries and more thunder along its tarmac as they travel between Leeds and Manchester. Up on the Pennine moorlands, the motorway reaches its highest point, and the Pennine Way walker gets an even higher place from which to admire it all. A simple but elegant footbridge bridge carries walkers over, 20m above the road. We weren't the only ones crossing over the motorway. It may have been a wet and murky Sunday in May, however there were more than enough people around for the bridge to be quite busy.

After a brief foray into Yorkshire, the Pennine Way re-entered Greater Manchester again (look, let's not get into that argument again) as it headed along Blackstone Edge; a gritstone escarpment with plenty of wet rocks to slip and slide around on.

The lack of sun, coupled with the darkness of the

rocks and boulders gave everywhere a grey and gloomy feel, and even a white painted trig point did little to cheer the place up. Cemented boldly onto a large lump of stone, it would surely be a contender for the top spot of any compiler's "Top 10 incongruous trig points of the world" list.

Several of the rocks had also faced some less official vandalism. Many a reckless youth had headed several miles up in the middle of nowhere in order to chisel their name into one; most noticeably by one E Crossfield who appeared to have made their mark on several rocks in 1924. Hooligans, the lot of them. If the ninety year old E Crossfield is still with us, I hope the police will be knocking on his door soon.

Nearby was a stone that was even older. The exact reasons why the Aiggin Stone was erected are lost in time, but it's believed by most that the simple gritstone pillar – emblazoned with a cross and the initials IT – marked the county boundary on an old packhorse route that was the M62 of its day.

In time the road was routed further downhill, where shelter could be more easily found. It even gained a number – the A58 – and is home to the White House pub. Originally opened in the 17th century, it's a popular spot with motorists and even the odd Pennine Way walker too.

That's not massively surprising. The pub's white buildings shine out like a beacon on the gloomy wet day, and given the weather, it was hard to ignore its welcoming door. Ignore it though we did, plodding on in the ever increasing rain, as the Pennine Way snaked its way alongside the Little Hazzles and Warland Reservoirs; the duo busy collecting the water for later distribution to the people of nearby Rochdale and Oldham.

Despite the damp weather, we were being passed by a never ending parade of people heading in the opposite direction, most of whom were decked in flimsy waterproofs and soggy looking trainers; large groups, families, sullen teenagers who had clearly been dragged away from the TV or their games console. Thirty odd people walked past us. Then forty, fifty and more. What were all these people doing wandering around in the rain on a wet and miserable Sunday afternoon?

Naturally, I could have asked. But that's not the kind of thing you do. Instead, we just let them pass by as they stomped around in the mud, pretending to have fun. Later we did find out what they were up to. This was the Todmorden Boundary Walk, an annual charity outing organised by the local Rotary Club. Those taking part had the option of covering the full 22 miles of the boundary, taking a mere ten and a half hours, or of walking the slightly more manageable Pike Walk which came in at a mere 12 miles in five hours instead.

As the rain came down, I began to picture the discussions that would have happened a few hours earlier. They would no doubt have involved statements like "Come on, it will be fun!" somewhere along the way.

At least the boundary walkers didn't have much

further to go; the end was in sight for them, which was more than it was for us. For us the warm, welcoming embrace of our B&B was a fair few miles yet. And first we had to head to the place the boundary walkers had just hiked from.

* * *

By itself Stoodley Pike isn't that impressive a hill, although it does offer a decent view of the surrounding area. What makes it stand out from its neighbours is the large monument stood on its top.

Work on the appropriately named Stoodley Pike Monument began in 1814. It was planned to celebrate the surrender of Napoleon Bonaparte and Paris during the Napoleonic Wars. Quite why the residents of nearby Todmorden felt so strongly that this was event would be best commemorated by erecting a large stone monument on a windswept hill, is another question entirely, but they did. However, the thing about building a monument to Napoleon surrendering and peace being restored in Europe is, that it all became moot when Napoleon then escapes his imprisonment and returned to power. Tools were naturally downed until Napoleon was had the ultimate defeat at the Battle of Waterloo. With him finally out of the equation, work on the monument was finally completed.

That wasn't the end of the tale though. Lightning and poor weather saw the monument collapse in 1854, which you may think would have been enough for everyone to simply give it all up as a bad job. Undeterred though, the locals spent two years repairing it. Further work took place in 1889, including the addition of a lightning conductor, and the whole thing has been standing there rather solidly ever since.

The best feature about Stoodley Pike Monument though is that you can go inside, which is exactly what we did. The monument's 39 steps take you up to a small viewing platform, a mere 12 metres above the ground, and only a third of the way up the monument. The staircase isn't lit, so much of the climb up is done in the dark; fun when all the concrete steps are slippery and wet, and I can tell you. But what a view it was. That short rise in height provided a splendid panorama. Well, until mist began to appear.

* * *

Back down on the ground, muddy paths and tracks led us the final few miles to Hebden Bridge. Or at least as close to Hebden Bridge as the Pennine Way dares to go. The trail doesn't like to get too near, sticking to the eastern outskirts, and requiring the walker who is in search of the town's many facilities to head a mile down the Rochdale Canal to get to Hebden Bridge proper.

Hebden Bridge is the few large towns on the Pennine Way, and most certainly the most distinctive of the group. Originally growing in the 18th century as a mill town, with a focus on the manufacturing of clothes, during the 1970s and

1980s the town became home to a sizeable community of artists, writers and photographers. We wouldn't pass through any other towns on our travels that featured vegetarian cafés, arts centres, community gardens, arty murals along the side of the canal, and an independent cinema.

Posters plastered around the town revealed that comedian and writer Robert Newman – once part of a double act with David Baddiel, and a quarter of the seminal 1990s sketch show, The Mary Whitehouse Experience – would be visiting as part of his nationwide tour. It turned out that our B&B too fitted in with the writing theme, as the landlady's husband was a foreign correspondent for a broadsheet newspaper. The walls of the house were filled with photographs of said journalist standing in a wide variety of far flung locations.

With all this culture on our doorstep, we did what any self-respecting walker would do. We went to the pub. This, to be fair, is better than some, for at least we spent the evening in the town. When writer Mark Wallington arrived in the town on his own Pennine Way journey, he hopped on a bus to Bradford for a curry instead.

But later on in the evening we took a stroll through the town, poking down its many nooks and crannies, falling slightly in love with its hippy-ish charms. Were it not for the fact that our next day's B&B was already booked and the deposit paid for, maybe we would never have left. Well, who could turn down the charms of Rob Newman?

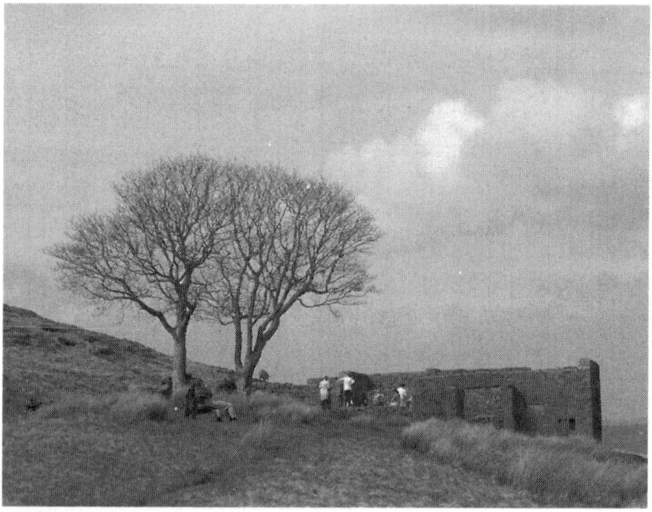

Hebden Bridge to Ponden

Catherine was hobbling. The past three days of walking had taken their toll on one of her knees; a problem I knew well from a couple of summers earlier when we'd been walking up and down hills and mountains of the Queyras Alps in France.

Dodgy knees can be a bit of a problem when you're on a walking holiday. In the Alps we'd had to pretty much abandon a whole day of walking thanks to the fact that the only way I could move without being in distinct agony, was to shuffle around very slowly. Instead of going up on an epic adventure to the top of a snow topped mountain, we ended up wandering around near a river, walking a few miles to get to our B&B. Even that took most of the day.

When we did make it to the village we were staying in, we decided to celebrate by taking a chair lift up a very tall hill to admire the panoramic view of Monte Viso from the top. It was pretty stunning, but on arrival back at the chair lift station we found the place distinctly closed; the doors bolted and the chair lift completely stopped, with the chairs swinging silently in the evening breeze.

We were several hundred metres above the town with the only way down (that we knew of anyway) being to walk down a (thankfully snow free) ski run. The result was a very slow hour as I stumbled, frequently swore and occasionally cried with every painful downward step. By some miracle I was perfectly fine the next day, although to this day, I've absolutely no idea how. Even so, as a precautionary measure, we purchased a pair a walking poles as soon as we could.

Yes, knees can be a problem, although since the Alps we'd tracked down a cure. One that seemed to be rather miraculous, and never failing. And it came in a white tube emblazoned simply with the words "Ibuprofen Gel."

I'm no doctor, but I have been told that knee problems are often caused by inflammation, something the drug Ibuprofen can swiftly cure. All we needed to do was slap some gel on Catherine's leg and she'd be fine. Since discovering this, we'd always tried to keep a tube with us in the small first aid kit that was usually stowed at the bottom of our pack, but it turned out we'd left it at home. Thank goodness though that we discovered the omission whilst we were in a large town. It could be easily solved by a visit to the nearby Co-Op. One swift purchase and a hasty slathering of sticky gel on the offending body part later, and within half an hour Catherine was ready to tackle anything the Pennine Way had to throw at us.

Which was rather useful as we had some hill climbing to do.

* * *

Hebden Bridge is nestled in a valley, which means,

rather inevitably, that the Pennine Way leaves the town by going up a hill. Up, up and up we went, zig-zagging along narrow streets and tracks as we gently rose above the Calder Valley. Half way up a sign gave us the option of following the "Wainwright Route", but with no idea where Alfred Wainwright's variation would take us, we stuck with the official version. I was none the wiser when I got home and consulted a copy of his book, Pennine Way Companion, either.

Pry Hill, Low Pillings and Hebble Hole all followed; the hole being a local beauty spot next to a stream that looked like a rather pleasant place to while away some hours whilst having a leisurely picnic. Less so on a rather grey and gloomy day, although still worthy of the few minutes we stopped there to munch on a flapjack.

Most of the day passed in a whirl of heather topped moorland; the kind with the slightly wet paths that, if anything, sums up the Pennine Way in a nutshell. Were anyone to ask me in the pub to describe a typical Pennine Way scene, the answer would probably include the words "wild looking moorland" somewhere in it.

I'd probably add "indistinct" to that sentence as well. Regularly the moors would look almost identical; browning, dry looking grass, clumps of heather and the odd grassy path or stream. And the Pennine Way does cross a fair amount of it. Once you got away from the green fields and the dry stone walls, and entered the heart of the moors, there often wasn't much to distinguish between them. Maybe someone with more knowledge of fauna and flora will want to correct me here, pointing out how the variety of cotton grass varies as you move the country, or something. But to me it all had a tendency to blur into one.

If it wasn't moorland we were crossing, then there were more of the inevitable reservoirs to walk along. And all this in relative peace and tranquillity. There was barely a sound to be heard other than the occasional bleating of a sheep, or the odd bird tweeting. It was a Bank Holiday but we had seen very few people since we'd left the bright lights of Hebden Bridge. Perhaps everyone was out for a celebratory pub lunch instead.

And so it was until, all of a sudden, a ruined farmhouse changed everything.

The buildings at Top Withens haven't been occupied since 1926, which explains why the main farmhouse has no roof. Despite this, the place was in remarkably good nick. Yes, there may be grass where the kitchen used to be, and the window panes were long gone. On the other hand, all the walls were in perfect condition and there wasn't a single bit of rubble to be found, giving the place the impression that someone had turned up one day, ripped off the roof, smashed in the windows and then very neatly cleared everything up before replacing the carpets with some new turf, before disappearing off again.

The answer to why this should be so, can be best found in a simple stone plaque attached to the walls of former building:

> "This farmhouse has been associated with 'Wuthering Heights', the Earnshaw home in Emily Brontë's novel. The buildings, even when complete, bore no resemblance to the house she described, but the situation may have been in her mind when she wrote of the moorland setting of the Heights.
>
> —Brontë Society 1964. This plaque has been placed here in response to many enquiries."

That there is absolutely no known connection between the farmhouse ruins and Emily Brontë's only novel doesn't stop hundreds and thousands of visitors heading up to Top Withens every year to pay homage. And it's not just Brits visiting either. Such is the draw of this remote place to the population of one particular nation, that the trek from a nearby car park is fully signposted in Japanese.

The only thing I knew about Wuthering Heights was Kate Bush's near magical début single, based on the novel. To me Top Withens was just an old building, with a lot of people poking about it, trying to work out where the cooker might have been originally. Dutifully we joined them in that poking, noting with vague interest where there would have been a connecting door, and wondering if the architects had heard about this novel thing called a ceiling, as it would be a useful thing to keep the rain out.

There's only so much interest a semi-abandoned building can give though – especially when you've never read the novel that certainly wasn't based on the place we were standing at – so we quickly left the crowds to their Mecca and headed onwards. The Pennine Way now followed a rather substantial path, designed no doubt to allow a coach load of tourists to do the stroll up the hill. There's dedication in that journey – a six or seven mile round trip from the nearest car park. And then when they reached the highlight of their pilgrimage would be reading a rather terse and dismissive plaque that basically chastised them for bothering. A result which seems fantastically British.

A reservoir was our destination, and on its edge, the welcoming embrace of Ponden House where our beds for the night could be found. We were welcomed in, and duly dispatched to the living room with a giant pot of tea and a plate of homemade biscuits, whilst various members of the landlady's family popped in to say hello.

"Are you having tea here tonight?" asked one, who had explained they were all up for a family visit. "My mum's an excellent cook."

We revealed that we weren't. Knowing the nearest pub to be a mile away, and having heard about Ponden House's fine reputation for an evening meal, we'd asked about it when booking, only to be told by the owner that she couldn't do them on Mondays as she went to an evening class.

"People do evening classes on a Bank Holiday Monday?" I'd said at the time, and as it turned out, the answer wasn't that they didn't. Not this evening class anyway. However, with no evening meal booked, an evening stroll down the road to the Old Silent Inn was in order.

The pub's rather curious name is supposedly derived from the 18th century, when Bonnie Prince Charlie is reputed to have hid out there for several weeks. Despite the fact that there was a 30,000 guinea reward for his capture, the locals kept silent about the Prince's location. Although their decision to do so might have had more to do with the fact that the lovely old Bonnie Prince had threatened to have their tongues cut out if they did so, rather than the locals having any real support for his cause. Still, silent they were and after the prince had left the pub was renamed after the fact that everyone had held (and kept) their tongues.

The pub had clearly been extended over the years, with plenty of room for the inevitable large groups that must surely pass by on the Brontë tourist trail. But with those visitors in their lodgings, the place was rather quiet, allowing us to spread out and relax with our pints before that difficult mile walk back to our lodgings.

The evening light was fading as we hobbled lazily around the reservoir, staring at the blues and pinks from the sky, reflected on the water's surface. It was a fine sight; a joy to look at and made all the finer by the knowledge that most visitors to the area would probably never get to see it.

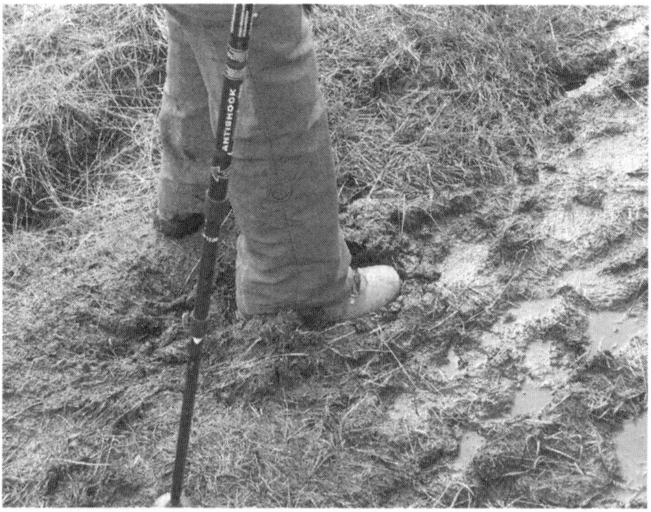
ARTISHOOK

Ponden to Earby

Walk the Pennine Way and inevitably you'll have a lot of fried breakfasts. Eggs, bacon and sausage will be a core feature of pretty much every B&B's breakfast menu; the only difference will be what else adorns the plate, and the quality of the ingredients.

Both can vary enormously. Will there be black pudding or not? Tomatoes, beans or both? Is the bread from a packet, or is it homemade? Proper home cooked hash browns, made with grated potato, or those strange, rather naff triangular things you find in the frozen food section of the supermarket. Will the sausages be at least 80% meat, or will they be those cheap ones that are bright pink, full of rusk and which will leave you feeling bloated all day?

After every walking trip we'd always end up reminiscing about the breakfasts on the journey home; ranking each one against each other. The good, the bad and the ugly. The ugly such as one B&B in Scotland we visited once when doing the West Highland Way where the proprietor proudly told us that she'd cooked the whole thing the night before and simply microwaved it in the morning. Even the fried egg. "You can't tell the difference," she enthusiastically told us. I held my counsel, but my taste buds begged to differ. Although given she talked ten to a dozen, it would have been a minor miracle if I'd ever managed to get a word in edgeways in order to complain. Even trying to ask to pay the bill took me half an hour whilst she rabbited on about local employment issues, clothes shopping and her holiday cottage on Skye.

With the Pennine Way being as long as it is, we inevitably had a lot of breakfasts to compare and rate. Most were merely fine, and none were truly terrible. But two stood out as being utterly fantastic. And one of them was Ponden House.

Everything about it was just superb; good quality food which was cooked perfectly. But the star was the potatoes. No frozen hashed browns here. In their place there was a side order of new potatoes, cut in half and gently pan fried. It was simply the perfect set up for another day of walking. If every Pennine Way breakfast had been that good, the trail would be gastronomic heaven.

Months later, inevitably sitting in a pub beer garden, we idly pondered sending out some sort of "Best Breakfast on the Pennine Way" award certificate. And nearly did, before deciding that a) it would probably be a bit too naff, and b) it was all a bit too much hassle.

* * *

With barely a cloud in the sky, we hoisted our packs on our backs, bade Ponden a fond farewell and set off for Thornton-in-Craven. The path skirted the side of the nearby reservoir, before taking us slowly and gently uphill. Fields and walls lined our way, until we hit Ikornshaw Moor where we were in for more miles of heather-topped moorland.

Occasional pools of peaty water glistened in the morning sun as we strode enthusiastically over the wide slab-paved path. Like Black Hill, this was another section that must be far easier to walk along now that the paving stones have gone down. No doubt prior to their installation, there would have been a fair amount of jumping over massive sections of bog required in order to get traverse the moor.

Once again we had the trail mostly to ourselves, but as we approached the edge of Ikornshaw Moor we spotted a pair of walkers carrying rather hefty rucksacks, wrapped with identical dark blue covers. They were clearly carrying camping gear – or, alternatively, enough food for a small army – and they scuttled around ahead of us, occasionally popping in and out of view like some sort of mirage. There was something almost beetle-like about their silhouettes in the sun. They turned out to not be insects, but a couple of walkers from the Netherlands, as we discovered when we greeted them as they rested against a dry stone wall. Although we never did find out why, of all the places they could have gone, they'd headed up onto the moors of Yorkshire.

Unlike its compatriots on the Pennine Way, Ikornshaw Moor did at least have some distinctive features in the form of a series of buildings, close to the northern side of the moorland. Some were well built and very solid looking, constructed out of stone and slate and well able to survive a cold winter. Others had a more rickety feel to them, made out of corrugated iron; rather flimsy and looking for all intents and purposes like a mild wind would blow them over. Whatever the building material, and the standard of their construction, they all shared a common element; their windows were all boarded up.

From the outside there was no obvious reason for them being there, and no clue to their existence could be found in our normally comprehensive guidebook. Presumably they were bothies and shelters of some kind, but the purpose of them was a mystery.

After a long trek, the moorland gave way to farming country; grassy pastures lined by dry stone walls and occupied by sheep. Coming down to the village of Ikornshaw, our guide book tempted us with mentions of the Black Bull Inn; a famous and popular Pennine Way drinking spot. Or, at least, it was. There'd be no welcoming landlord to serve us a well-kept pint of real ale. And whilst we could pull a chair up to a table, if we did we'd be doing so in the furniture showroom that now occupied the building. Those now requiring liquid refreshment, rather than a new sofa were now required to walk a mile or so up to the road to the neighbouring village of Cowling.

Opportunities for lunchtime drinks were generally rare on the Pennine Way, although that was probably for the best. One pint never seems enough, yet two is at lunchtime will inevitably make the rest of the day go rather slowly. Besides, there was always beer a-plenty in the evening; the fact that a walking trail in England rarely ends the day without the ability to sup a nice pint is, after all, one of the benefits of walking here.

Still, in this case we were out of luck, so instead we began the climb out of the village, pausing at the corner of an attractive looking field, with plenty of shade from the sun, where we scoffed our packed lunch.

In a break from the usual routine, the Pennine Way now took us through fields and down deserted country lanes for a couple of miles, with a brief interlude through the sleepy village of Lothersdale. Lothersdale had managed to keep hold of its pub, and as we passed there were some people sat outside supping pints. People who stared at us intently, their eyes following us as we walked up the main street. Either we were the most exciting thing they'd seen all week, or the pub's regulars weren't keen on new people. It was hard to know for sure, and to be honest it was almost a relief to be back on the wild looking, heather topped moorland once more.

With no bog to navigate, Elslack Moor instantly won a couple of fans. No peat bog meant there were no paving slabs; just a gentle and relaxing grassy path weaving its way through the brown heather. The only serious challenge was the odd patch of deep mud, which oozed and groaned under the weight of a human being and their hiking boot.

For the most part, the Pennine Way headed along the edge of the moorland, separated from the lush green grass of the neighbouring field by the inevitable line of dry stone walls. And before long, the moors ended and we entered into those same kind of fields as we got close to the village of Thornton-in-Craven.

For the Pennine Way walker, Thornton had a distinct flaw. It has no pub, and no B&B. Which means that those seeking accommodation and refreshment need to head elsewhere, which for us meant a detour to Earby, a couple of miles off route.

On the face of it, it looked like the way to get there would be to walk down the A56 road, but close inspection of our Ordnance Survey map showed an old railway line, which the Pennine Way crossed over near the remnants of Thornton's old railway station. There was no right of way noted on the map, but it went to the right place in a more direct route than the road. All we needed to know was whether we could actually get down it.

Trying to use it was a gamble, but on approaching the old trackbed it was pretty clear that it was well used by locals, even if to use it they needed to pass by a distinctly ominous warning sign.

> "Warning. This private land is dangerous. Persons use it at their own risk and the County Council will accept no liability for any injury or damage resulting in such use."

Eyebrows were raised. Especially as the county council in question appeared to be Lancashire, meaning we'd crossed out of the land of the white rose without realising it.

That aside, the question was what was so dangerous about this former railway line? What was so sinister about it that Lancashire County Council saw fit to put this sign up, and why did they think that people might sue them over use of private land, presumably not owned by them? It was a sign that just posed further questions. Still, there were a lot of people using the track so we decided to risk it whilst being ever alert for the extreme danger that surely waited for us.

For a 'dangerous path', it was amazingly short of danger. It was so threatening to life and limb that several neighbouring fields had stiles in their fences, so that you could get easier access to this source of potential injury. Still, I kept my eyes peeled, constantly searching the land for anything that result in a broken arm, or a sprained ankle. But the most alarming thing I could see was a block of wood with a small metal hinge on it. It was so far off the path that the chances of it harming anyone were next to zero. A tree stump could have done more damage to someone. Based on that, it was hard to work out why it simply hadn't been made a formal right of way like so many other disused railway tracks in the country.

* * *

We were staying in Earby's YHA, tucked away on the far side of town down, and were greeted with a warm welcome by the warden who told us he'd "upgraded" us from a two bed room to exclusive use of a full dorm "so you have plenty of space to spread out in." Although his follow up comment of "Also, the bigger rooms are easier for me to clean!" may just have revealed his true motives.

After dutifully admiring the room we'd been given (and its six bunk beds), we set off down the road to the Red Lion pub, parking up in the empty pub lounge, from where we ordered an epic feast to fill our bellies. Dessert was even part of the main course, thanks to the side-salad on each dish including raspberries.

As we ate and drank, the pub got busier, mainly thanks to a large group of women who began to arrive in dribs and drabs. Given the looks in our direction, with the occasional "Oh!" of surprise, we were obviously sitting in their preferred spot in the pub's lounge, although they soon found a new home at the other end of the small room.

As we left, I wondered what they'd be saying to each other now that they had the place to themselves. Was the air filled with comments of "Oh, thank goodness they've gone," before everyone rushed to the newly vacant table? Or did in later weeks, find themselves sitting elsewhere in the pub? Maybe our interlude would see them introduced to the merits at sitting closer to the bar, rather than next to the door. Perhaps we'd have to go back and find out.

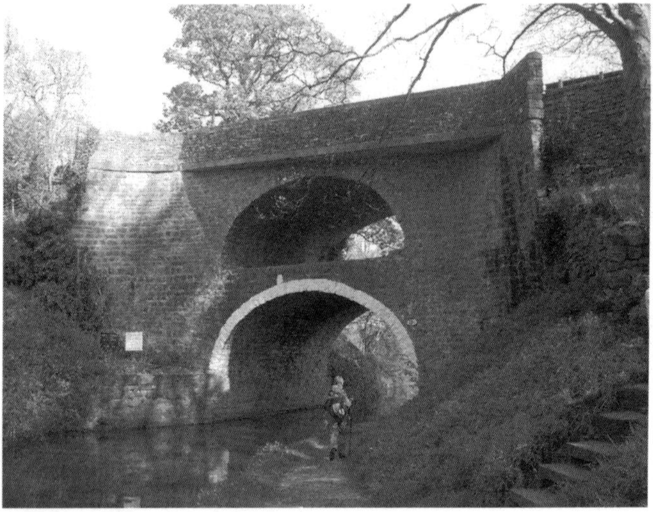

Earby to Gargrave

The more you walk of the Pennine Way, the greater the sense of familiarity there is about it. It is a walk through the Pennines after all; it is a trail that follows a major geographical feature, which means that when all is said and done, things aren't going to change that much as you head along.

It doesn't matter which section you're doing because you'll see similar things. You can pretty much guarantee that your day will include some heather-topped moorland up on a hill, some dry stone walls, a reservoir and a few sheep staring at you in bafflement. As you head north, then the reservoirs decrease a little, as do the number of busy roads, however forests and woodland get added into the mix. But still, there's a set of familiar themes: hills, heather, dry stone walls, reservoirs and sheep. Especially the sheep.

Which is why, when you have a day on the Pennine Way that doesn't conform to the rules, then you suddenly find yourself rather confused.

Earby to Gargrave was of those days.

With just six or so miles to walk, our journey to Gargrave was never going to be particularly taxing. We had just one requirement: to get there at lunchtime. Gargrave had a railway station, and home – and, by implication, gainful employment – beckoned back in London. The trains were infrequent and we'd need to be there in time to catch the local stopping service to Leeds, from where we'd change to an inter-city service to the capital.

Six miles before lunchtime? More than doable if we got on our way early enough. And as Earby hostel was self-catering only, there'd be no delay caused by waiting for breakfast. Although this did mean our early morning subsistence consisted mainly of a cereal bar purchased from a newsagent which was the only shop in Earby which seemed to open at 8am.

We double backed up the old railway line to Thornton-in-Craven, once again managing not to break an arm, fracture our skull or indulge in any other activity that might lead us to vaguely consider legal action against Lancashire County Council. Seriously, the thought hadn't even crossed my mind to do so until they stuck a massive great big sign up. Anyway, back on the Pennine Way, we set off on a day of walking that would defy the Pennine Way's conventions.

Okay, okay. So there were sheep. Plenty of them. And yes, there were dry stone walls everywhere. However, in my defence, there was no heather to be found and not a single reservoir to be seen either. And as for moorland...

Now I know what you're thinking. You're thinking "Andrew, you're only walking for a half a day. Surely if you did a full day of walking, you'd see all those things?!" To which the answer is no, you wouldn't. A full day of walking would take you to Malham. And there's no heather, no major hills and no reservoirs to be seen on the stretch to there from Gargrave either.

It was like the Pennines had just stopped. Which, of course, they hadn't. They were just a bit thin on the ground at this point. And those hills that there were, weren't where the Pennine Way wanted to go. Which meant the day – well morning anyway – would be spent in luscious green fields, filled with frolicking lambs.

And not far on from Thornton-in-Craven, there was a stretch that was so un-Pennine Way like that it was unbelievable.

We found ourselves walking on a canal tow path.

The Leeds and Liverpool canal wasn't the first the Pennine Way had met – we'd crossed over one at Hebden Bridge – but this was the first time that the trail actually followed a canal.

It felt weird. Distinctly wrong. And it was a mercy when the canal curved off, and the Pennine Way took a more direct path to Gargrave through some fields instead. But that was after it passed under the impressive double arch bridge at East Marton.

The bridge – a bit of a local landmark in this part of farming country – was basically created by plonking one arch on top of another. The bridge originally consisted of just the lower arch, however when it was built the bridge was at a lower level than the road. Eventually it was decided to raise the bridge up to be the same height as the road. And why build a whole new bridge when you could re-use part of what you already had? Hence, the builders simply put a second arch on top of the first.

* * *

The last few miles passed in a blur of fields as the village of Gargrave came into view. Sitting on the edge of the Yorkshire Dales National Park, it's a popular spot for visitors, as witnessed by the crowds lining the Dalesman Café Tearooms at the heart of the village. And before we knew it, we were inside scoffing a cream tea. So what if it was only 11am? Let's face it, there's never a bad time to munch a jam and cream-laden scone.

With quite some time to fill before our train departed, we eked out every last bit of tea from the pot, and dutifully admired the café's shelves of sweets at the front of the shop; all stored and served from old fashioned looking glass jars. Even the chocolate bars were given a star treatment, arranged in an antique wooden rack emblazoned with "Cadbury's Milk Chocolate" in elaborate writing.

I could have bought everything in the shop – except the liquorice as I can't stand the stuff – but I feared for my teeth. So instead, we set forth to the station only a mere half an hour before our train arrived.

Alas, there's only so much amusement you can get from railway stations. During our wait, I read all of the posters at least once – especially the one informing me I must have a valid ticket, which thankfully I did have. Once I'd done with that, there really was little to do other that sit on a bench and wait and look back on the journey we'd done. Edale to Gargrave was now completed. A quarter of the Pennine Way had been walked. Which, for six days effort, really was not bad at all.

Part 2

Gargrave to Horton-in-Ribblesdale
First trip walking the Pennine Way

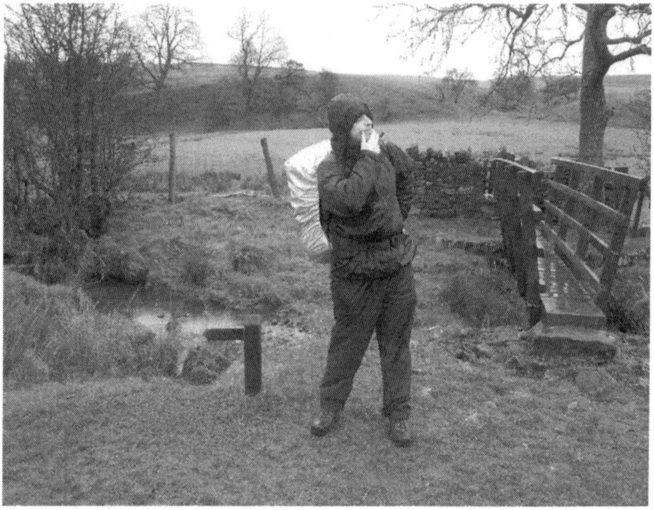

Gargrave to Malham

We left Gargrave just over a year before we'd arrived there, which may sound a bit meta-physical, but is the reality of the situation.

The fact is that whilst most people start a walk at the beginning, we started the Pennine Way about a third of the way through. But then we also we'd arrived at Gargrave having never intended to actually walk the whole of the Pennine Way. The plan was simply to walk it for a day and a half up to Horton-in-Ribblesdale, then spend a day in the Horton area exploring the local fells. There was no grand vision, no master plan. Only at the end of the trip would we realise that walking that short stretch of the Pennine Way would lead us to doing the whole thing; that we'd accidentally embarked on some bigger quest. Instead, it was just intended to be merely a long weekend away; a chance to get out of London and into the clean air of Yorkshire's countryside.

We'd spent the evening before in Leeds, catching up with an old university friend of mine who had settled in the city for work purposes. We'd been to the pub, had an insanely long chat and then ended up having a rather early night thanks to the fact that Jen had an early start the next morning. Which was also why we found ourselves standing at Leeds's main train station at the unearthly hour of

6:30 in the morning with nearly two hours to kill before the first train left for Gargrave.

Now I don't know if you've ever been to Leeds train station but if you haven't, frankly there's barely enough to keep you interested for fifteen minutes at the best at time. At half six, there was nothing to do other than watch a handful of people who were darting off to the platforms to catch a train. The only moment that caused even a stir came at seven when the station's branch of Wetherspoon's opened, and then that only registered with two people; namely the pair of us as it meant we could get something to eat for breakfast. Let's just say that the moment that we could board a rather rickety train and get on out of the city, was met with much rejoicing.

We spent much of the journey watching the rain hit the train windows, struggling with our waterproofs and doing the best to attach unfamiliar rucksack covers to our packs; mentally preparing ourselves for what was to come.

And on that front, I really had little idea.

Despite growing up a few miles from the trail, I knew next to nothing about the Pennine Way. It was just a squiggle on a map. Although as I learned later, the stretch we were about to cover to Horton would hardly be the most representative of the whole thing.

For instead of the heather-topped moorland with its peaty pools of water, this section to the village of Malham was firmly spent either in farmland or next to the River Aire. There were few major viewpoints and the little excitement that there was, came in the form of a dead sheep which lay at the edge of a snow covered Eshton Moor. And that was about it. Indeed, looking at Wainwright's Pennine Way Companion now as I type, it's noticeable that even he struggled to come up with much to say. Whilst I haven't done a detailed word count, the four pages dedicated to travelling between Gargrave and Malham do seem far lighter on text than most of the other pages. And about a third of what he did write and draw was dedicated to Gordale Scar which isn't actually on the Pennine Way, but which Wainwright flags as a "recommended detour."

That's not to say that this was a pleasant walk. Far from it. However, it is what it is. A walk through some fields and down a river. Although I can't guarantee a dead sheep will be there if you visit.

* * *

The rain was a theme for most of the morning; the River Aire was heavily swollen and gushing merrily. Walking in the rain is rarely fun. There's little on a walk that can be more down-heartening than having to put your head down to stop the stuff going in your eyes, whilst you rustle and sweat in your waterproofs. At least it wasn't particularly heavy – just ever present – and we managed to push on with a smile. Even the odd navigational errors which would see Catherine lead me confidently up a hill for several minutes, before pausing, glaring at the map then quietly adding "I think that wasn't the right way" before going down again, didn't dampen our spirits.

The Pennine Way meandered along, passing by villages and hamlets with curious names. Airton. Kirby Malham. Hanlith. In one – who knows which, for they all looked quite similar – we sat on a bench on the edge of a tiny village green and ate apples, presumably looking like a bunch of escaped lunatics to the locals peering at us from behind their net curtains. Only a fool would be out in this weather, after all.

And then, all of a sudden, we were in Malham, standing outside the warm embrace of the Buck Inn with six and a half miles under our belt. It had gone like a blur, although that was maybe due to restricted vision caused by the hoods on our waterproof jackets.

We stood for a moment, taking in our surroundings as a large party of school children marched past in identical maroon coloured waterproofs. The village was otherwise deserted.

The pub's hikers bar was closed; for some reason there wasn't enough demand for it on a soggy Thursday lunchtime in March. I can't imagine why not. Still, the main bar was open and that was good enough for us, and leaving our extremely wet hiking boots by the main door, we sauntered inside.

"I'll light the fire to help you dry out," came the call from behind the bar as the barman caught us struggling out of wet clothing.

For that comment alone, I could have hugged him. Before we knew it, we were sitting next to a roaring fire – our clothes spread over the chairs of most of the surrounding tables – watching as water slowly dripped out of our sodden gloves as they hung up in front of the log fire.

As we dried out, the barman told us he was contemplating getting his waterproofs on and heading out to the hills himself later in the afternoon. Looking outside at the rain and then to my pint of ale, I personally had a strange compulsion to stay indoors.

* * *

The children were trooping past again as we struggled into our still wet boots in the pub's doorway. I idly wondered if they'd actually been anywhere at all, or had just spent their whole day marching up and down Malham's small main street like a bunch of extras from a film set. At least they were now doing it in dry weather; the rain having finally stopped in the time it had taken me to digest a prawn cocktail baguette and a couple of pints of ale.

We didn't have far to go. We were going no further on the Pennine Way for the day, and our B&B was only a few minutes up the road. However there was that "recommended detour" of Wainwright's to visit.

Malham – it must be said – has more than its fair share of natural wonders. It is perhaps best known for the mighty Malham Cove, and the spectacular limestone pavement on top of it. However, as we'd be passing that way the following morning on the Pennine Way, we instead headed off the trail in order to see its other star attractions: Janet's Foss and Gordale Scar.

The two sit not far from each other, and are usually accessed by following a simple walking trail from Malham; the route's popularity confirmed by the robust path that took us alongside fields, and through the woodlands of the Malham Tarn Estate. The path looked like it could hold a coach party full of people, and perhaps in the summer it did. A damp day in Spring saw just a few less visitors making their way past the puddles.

As waterfalls go, Janet's Foss isn't exactly huge. It's actually pretty tiny. Were it not for its setting, it would probably get no attention at all. The water plunges down into a large pool, surrounded by trees and greenery. It's like walking into some sort enchanted forest; home to mythical beings and legendary creatures. Indeed, it's believed the waterfall's name is a reference to Jennet, a fairy queen who, folk tales tell, inhabited the small cave at the back of the waterfall. Over time Jennet became Janet and the rest is history. As for the foss bit, well that's more tangible. It's an old Nordic word, still used to describe a waterfall in Scandinavian countries. There aren't many fosses left in Britain; they've mostly changed to the more anglicised "Force" instead; several of which can be found on the Pennine Way itself. But here in

Malhamdale there was one waterfall that was firmly clinging onto the old ways.

Leaving the queen of the fairies to her peace, we followed another path on to Gordale Scar; a ravine with 100m tall limestone cliffs, which has a couple of waterfalls that Gordale Beck flows from the hill above, before it eventually joins the River Aire further down-stream.

For those that wanted to go further, the path carried on up the beck; a good scramble taking the walker in the narrow gap between the cliffs and the waterfalls. Follow the right paths and you can end up at the top of Malham Cove, before heading down to the pub for a pint. You might even get wet. Or more wet if you've been out in the rain. But with the afternoon getting on, it was far more sensible to head back the way we came. We didn't need an excuse to visit the pub after all, and there'd be plenty of time for walking the next day.

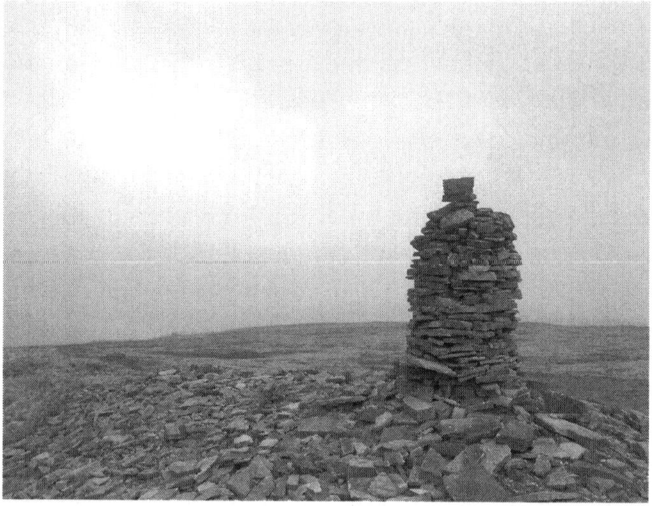

Malham to Horton-in-Ribblesdale

It seems to be the case that all travel writing needs to feature a quote from Bill Bryson in it somewhere. Doesn't matter quite where, but its inclusion is compulsory; because of a tradition, or an old charter or something. That is, unless you are Bill Bryson, for Bill Bryson quoting himself would be just a tad strange and weird. So if you're Bill Bryson, you need to quote Paul Theroux instead.

In case you haven't noticed, my name isn't Bill Bryson. This means that, according to the rules, I need to include something attributed to him somewhere in this tome. And in doing so, I had a choice. A prime candidate, and personal favourite, was his quote about looking like a giant condom when decked out in waterproofs. But instead I decided to go with this one:

> "I won't know for sure if Malhamdale is the finest place there is until I have died and seen heaven (assuming they let me at least have a glance), but until that day comes, it will certainly do."

Bill knew the Malhamdale area well, living locally for several years before he and his family left the UK in order to live in the United States. He did return, but not to Malhamdale. These days he lives in Norfolk.

Anyway, is Malhamdale the finest place there is? I don't feel like I've done enough research to be sure. Although, I confess that personally I'm inclined to put the Scottish Highlands above it. Still, it's a beautiful place, with some very fine features. And the Pennine Way was leading us directly towards two of them.

* * *

The first thing that springs to the lips on seeing Malham Cove is "wow." Probably quickly followed by "that's big." And it is. The Cove's cliff face is 80m high, and about 300m wide, and it sits there – just sits there – at the head of the valley. You stop, stare it at it for a while. And then you pose in front of it for a photograph whilst grinning like a loon.

You wander cautiously to the rock face, idly wondering where that stream is coming from. The one that just emerges from a hole at the bottom of the cliffs, and just flows on merrily. No waterfall here; this water is heading down from the top of the hill via a network of caves instead.

Then you realise that you have to go up to the top. Not because it's calling for you to climb it or anything. It's more that you've seen that Pennine Way signpost that sits to the side of the path, and it's pointing up a set of steps, which are going to take you up to the top. And where the Pennine Way goes, so must you. Besides, if you don't you'll find yourself at a dead end.

In terms of height, the ascent up those steps isn't particularly big, but it feels like it. You probably should go to the gym more. But up you go, pausing every now and then for a moment to admire the view of the valley. And catch your breath. And then, all of a sudden, you're at the top. And wow, was that rock face nothing – not one thing – in comparison to what you saw below, because now you're standing on top of Malham Cove's mighty limestone pavement.

The ground is covered in the stuff. Large blocks of limestone, with channels in between, looking like some sort of crazy paving scheme created by the local big friendly giant. One that was the result of him making a proper pavement but not being bothered to smooth it off by filling in the cracks. As a giant it probably doesn't make much difference to him or her, however you – being normal sized – are required to bounce around on top, bounce, bounce, bounce from limestone boulder to limestone boulder.

Then you make your way to the edge of the cliff to look down at that view. And oh my, what a view. There's the valley down there. There's where you walked the day before, and the panorama stretches miles further off into the distance. Unless the cloud is low, in which case you won't see much at all.

You potter around at the top of the pavement, looking at the nooks and crannies, wondering about it all; how it came to be (the answer is nothing to do with lazy giants, but instead due to the limescale being eroded by water over millions of years) before checking your watch and reluctantly dragging yourself away.

But that's all right because the limestone doesn't end there. Anyone walking here will find themselves heading up hill once more, through a craggy landscape. There are rocks everywhere, caves and even some sinkholes, where water from streams sinks through the limestone ground, eventually joining rivers some miles away.

Slowly but surely you begin to leave the limestone behind; grass begins to dominate and just for a minute you think it's all back to plain sailing. That the Pennine Way hasn't got anything else for you to admire.

Then you arrive at Malham Tarn. And your love for the area is renewed and bolstered further. For this lake – the highest in England, incidentally – looks near perfect too. And you pause and think that maybe that Bryson fellow was onto something after all.

* * *

A large Georgian manor house sits at the top of Malham Tarn, home to a field studies centre owned by the Field Studies Council. I wasn't entirely sure what the Field Studies Council did, but I was sure it was appropriate that the Pennine Way went right on its doorstep.

We weaved past the buildings and made our way on towards our next target: Fountains Fell, which would be the highest point of our journey so far.

Despite the height – Fountains Fell rises 668m above sea level – it was an easy climb thanks to a gently ascending path running over a couple of miles. Although, as Fountains Fell has a rather flat top there wasn't going to be much of a view when we got there. And that's before we took the weather into consideration. The sky was just full of haze and cloud, meaning there wasn't a view of much at all really.

We were walking through a former mining area, and coal pits and mine workings can be spotted by the observant all across the fell top. And then there were the shake holes – gaping holes in the ground, caused by water removing soil or bedrock – which we passed plenty of. Several were exceptionally large, certainly plenty big enough to fall down. No small wonder that many of them are popular with cavers.

Unfortunately for Fountains Fell, the crown of "The Highest Point on the Pennine Way, So Far" was to be swiftly taken away from it. Nearby Pen-y-ghent comes in at 26m higher and is the next port of call for the walker heading towards Kirk Yetholm. The haze meant we'd been unable to get much of a view of it from afar, however as we now got closer it began to emerge from the gloom.

To anyone who has seen it, Pen-y-Ghent must be one of the most instantly recognisable fells around. It's also one of the hardest shapes to describe. In for the challenge though, I got my notebook out and got thinking. Descriptions of sleeping cats or lions sprang to mind, as did up-turned pasta bowls. But in the end I decided that the shape of Pen-y-Ghent was like a big flat lump, with a nose carved out on one side; an image most people will be instantly able to conjurer up in a matter of seconds, I am sure.

Along with neighbouring Whernside and Ingleborough, Pen-y-Ghent is one of the "Three Peaks", although these days most people call them the Yorkshire Three Peaks; the original name having been, in recent years, nabbed to describe the ascent the challenge of walking Ben Nevis, Snowdon, and Scafell Pike all in one day. Well sorry guys, but Yorkshire got there first as far as I'm concerned.

The summit of Pen-y-Ghent is an ideal place to take in the view of the other neighbouring hills. Or at least should be. From the valley below it was quite clear that we wouldn't be seeing much at all. With so much cloud and haze in the area, Catherine had even pondered bailing out. What was the point in heading up a major hill like Pen-y-Ghent if there'd be no view from the top of it, she mused, before spending several minutes investigating alternative, non-hill based alternative routes to Horton-in-Ribblesdale.

To some, such an attitude would be sacrilegious. But why? The Pennine Way is just a path after all; a slightly arbitrary line drawn across the country that loosely follows a string of hills. Would it really matter that much if we skipped part of it because it wouldn't particularly be worth doing?

Well yes, of course it would. And that's exactly

why we headed up Pen-y-ghent. Up its stone steps and over its gravel paths. Higher and higher until, at long last, we reached the top. And found that there was next to no view to be seen. All that was visible was a few bits of Pen-y-ghent's slopes. Any chance of admiring the splendour of the neighbouring fells was thwarted.

We spent a few minutes enjoying the sheer novelty of being able to see absolutely nothing – a feat we'd get to enjoy several times more on later trips – and being battered by a strong wind that had appeared out of nowhere and which was hitting Pen-y-ghent as hard as it could.

"Maybe it will blow the cloud and haze away," said Catherine optimistically, although it seemed unlikely anything would be happening soon and we soon began to head down again.

It had been a pointless visit to the summit, but hey, at least the sanctity of the Pennine Way – and our pride – was intact.

* * *

Hull Pot is apparently – and I say apparently, because I can't actually find out who said it to be so – the largest pothole in Britain. It's 91 metres long, 18m wide and another 18m deep. It's got a waterfall in it, and very occasionally fills up completely with water. It sits just to the side of the Pennine Way and is a splendid sight; an awc inspiring, inspiration and one of the finest things a Pennine Way walker will see on the whole of their journey. Or so I'm told because we just walked right past the short detour to it without noticing.

We did at least admire nearby Horton Scar; another set of limestone rock faces like Malham Cove, although nowhere near as dramatic. Or maybe we just felt that because we were gasping for a cup of tea, and looking for excuses to move on. Either way, Horton Scar didn't quite get the same level of appreciation we'd shown to its fellow down in Malhamdale.

A cuppa was, at least, close by. Our two day trek on the Pennine Way would be ending just a short way down the track in the village of Horton-in-Ribblesdale. The Pennine Way entered the village's main street in triumph, arriving right outside the Pen-y-ghent Café. The café spends most of its time dishing out cups of tea and bacon rolls to walkers and over visitors, however its staff also find time to run a clocking-in service for those walkers trying to walk, or run, all three peaks in a day. Oh and it also doubles up as the local tourist information office.

The latter point was the handiest for us. We'd booked in for the night at the Crown Inn, one of the village's two pubs. There was a slight snag. We didn't know where it was. Both our guidebook and an information board near the café listed the The Golden Lion and the New Inn. The Crown Inn was completely absent from both.

The café was just closing up as two confused walkers entered, wondering whether they'd managed to book themselves into some pub in a completely different village by mistake. The man behind the counter was swift to reassure us. The mysterious New Inn was actually the Crown after all. The café's owner pointed us in the right direction, much to our relief.

"You're walking the Pennine Way then?" he said, before popping under the counter and bringing out a large notebook. "We have a signing in book for people walking it."

It was an understatement of epic proportions. For the Pen-y-ghent Café has the oldest known Pennine Way signing in book, which now spreads over several volumes.

"Oh we're not walking the whole thing," explained Catherine, worried that someone might the wrong idea about our intentions. The response was a shrug, and the proliferation of a pen, and our names were quickly added to the book.

She needn't have worried. Settling into the Crown's bar that evening, supping a pint of the gloriously dark, smooth and silky Theakston's Old Peculier, I muttered some words that would prove to be immortal.

"I could do some more of this Pennine Way thing."

It seemed that whilst our two day jaunt had ended, and the mission had begun.

Part 3

Horton-in-Ribblesdale to Dufton
Second trip walking the Pennine Way

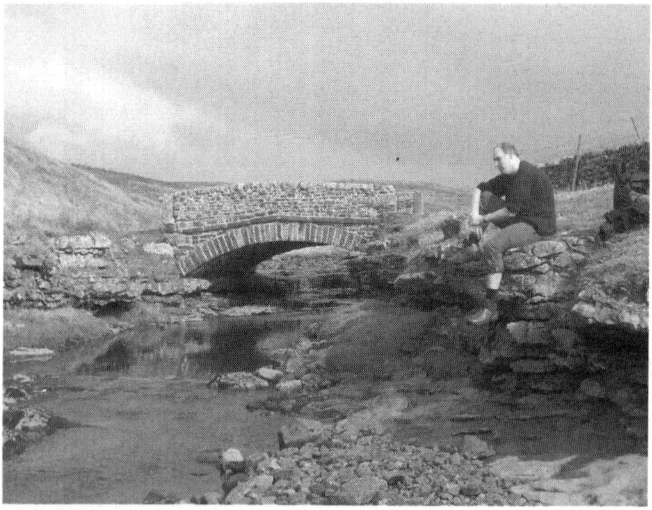

Horton-in-Ribblesdale to Hawes

We'd barely been back in London a few hours before the maps were being scoured over, railway timetables studied, guide books consulted and the old heads scratched as we attempted to plan our return to the Pennine Way.

Even so, it would be another six months before we arrived back in Horton-in-Ribblesdale again. We still hadn't quite committed ourselves to doing the whole thing; just to another four days on the trail which would take us up to Dufton. Still, it looked a promising route, which would allow us to visit a remote pub, and head out of Yorkshire, through Teesdale and into Cumbria where we'd see one of the finest sights on the whole of the Pennine Way.

After reacquainting ourselves with Horton's many sights – a process that took the whole of ten minutes – we set off again on a cool but distinctly sunny October morning. There were blue skies and those light wispy clouds that flutter and fluff along so neatly in the sky as we headed out of the village along a walled track; the three peaks of Pen-y-ghent, Ingleborough and Whernside dominating the skyline. There was even the odd glimpse of a train on the Settle to Carlisle line down across the valley, although hopes that billowing smoke from a steam engine would be visible on the horizon were dashed by the realisation that the line was mostly occupied by diesel engines pulling long freight trains.

The ground around the path seemed to be full of holes. We were in caving country, with plenty of gaps between rocks, spots where potholers could disappear off into gloom for their subterranean exploration. Sell Gill Holes is a particularly popular spot, where there is apparently a relatively accessible set of caves. Down there somewhere was a cavern 64m high, and at the entrance a stream flowed in. We stood there listening to the sound of the water crashing down to the cave floor, and at that point I knew it would take a hell of a lot to persuade me to crawl down through the narrow gap and into the depths of the earth. No, those cavers could keep it for themselves as far as I was concerned.

More limestone caves followed; more subtle entrances for those who get their kicks heading underground. Dry Laithe Cave even had a stream flowing into it, making its name perhaps a tad ironic. And then there was Ling Gill which wasn't a cave at all, but actually a limestone gorge, all lined with trees whose leaves were busily changing themselves to offer a display of Autumn's finest colours.

Nearby too sat Ling Gill Bridge, a small, slightly dumpy yet attractive 16th century stone construction which allowed people to cross the stream without getting their feet wet. And according to one guide book writer extraordinaire

Alfred Wainwright, it also marks a boundary between limestone and peat based moorlands. Well, if he says so. I was more interested in the fact that it was a lovely spot to rest awhile, which is exactly what we did, sitting on a rock and dangling our legs near the stream.

What it didn't offer though was a view of the mighty Ribblehead Viaduct. The figurehead of the Settle to Carlisle railway line, the twenty-four arch viaduct took a thousand navvies four years to build before being completed in 1894. Work was tough, with the navvies living with their families in shanty towns under the shadow of the viaduct. It's an amazing sight – more so when you consider it was built without all the modern building equipment we now take for granted – and consists of an estimated 1.5 million bricks, yet by the 1980s Ribblehead Viaduct was at the centre of a campaign to close the railway line completely.

British Rail had been running down the line for years, in a classic example of "closure by stealth", where the service was deliberately run down in order to make the line uneconomical. All but two stations on the line were closed in 1970, with just two passenger trains a day remaining. Repair work was cut back leaving viaducts and tunnels in poor condition, and freight services were diverted to use the West Coast mainline instead.

After years of being run-down, the closure notices finally went up in 1984; British Rail citing the huge cost of repairing the line and bringing it up to spec. At the heart of that were the quotes of astronomical proportions to complete the repair work on the Ribblehead Viaduct – a whopping £6m in itself.

But the line wasn't going to go down without a fight. Campaigners, including local authorities and rail enthusiasts, fought a bitter battle, citing the fact that the potential for tourism had been completely ignored, and that the line provided a useful diversionary route for the West Coast mainline. They were also helped on their way by the discovery that repair costs had been deliberately exaggerated.

It took five years, but the campaigners won. The final decision rested on the shoulders of a certain Minister for Transport and now TV presenter named Michael Portillo who rejected the application, later describing it as his greatest achievement in politics.

With the line saved, many of the old stations were re-opened and the vital repair work was completed at a far lower cost than originally estimated. Tourist traffic increased dramatically, however it is freight which is at the heart of the modern Settle to Carlisle line, carrying coal to power stations in Yorkshire.

Ribblehead Viaduct is without doubt a fine structure, although one that sadly the Pennine Way prefers to view only afar. Still, on a fine day a good view can be had of it, as it sits nestling in the hills. Unfortunately the weather wasn't working in our favour. After starting clearly, a dull haze was beginning to envelop our view leaving a magnificent viaduct, to be rendered a series of fuzzy blobs looming over the horizon.

* * *

The Pennine Way's most obvious connections with the Romans can be found at Hadrian's Wall, further up the trail. However, there are other Roman links, such as the several miles along the straight Cam High Road.

There are some Roman roads that you can follow and get a sense of their history; what it must have been like to be a centurion marching along in his sandals. And there are others where you could just be walking over any track, anywhere. Cam High Road fell firmly into the latter category, thanks to the fact that these days it mostly follows a dry stone wall. And if there's one thing that does rather prevent you from regressing to the Roman era, its walking alongside a dry stone wall.

And that wasn't all. Based on its condition, the track seemed to be well frequented by 4x4 drivers; perhaps more so than Pennine Way hikers. Like many old green lanes, Cam High Road was open to motor vehicles. Or at least, was on our visit. A year later 4x4 drivers were banned from using it after complaints that the old road had been wrecked by drivers. One thing is certain – whilst Cam High Road has survived many a thing, it was never designed up to cope with the onslaught of the off-road vehicle.

Our own journey was without any vehicular blight. In fact we'd barely seen anyone all day; our main source of company being a handful of sheep who were spread thinly over this wild and lonely looking hill. The hazy weather helped to make it feel even more remote; blocking off the view of the surrounding valleys and fields as it hovered in the air.

As it hit late afternoon and we got our first glimpse of the market town of Hawes, the haze began to be accompanied by dark clouds, which were providing a foreboding gloom about the place. A warning sign about a bull being in the field made things feel distinctly worse as we left the moorland for tracks through fields. Still, at least it was dry. But not for long; the rain finally began as we entered into the neighbouring village of Gayle via a small housing estate.

With waterproofs on we strode purposely into Hawes's bustling main street, lined with pubs, gift shops and vendors of antiques, cars, and coaches. The place was packed with visitors who had come from far and wide to check out the local attractions, which include the mighty Wensleydale dairy on the edge of the town. In sharp contrast to the rest of the day, we were close to fighting our way through the crowds in order to make it to Hawes's YHA.

The last time I'd stayed in a youth hostel was two nights spent in Ilam Hall hostel in Derbyshire when I was 12 years old, with other children from my primary school. An imposing old manor house with large dorms, the hostel had been ruled with an iron grip by the warden who barked out instructions to all and sundry, and diligently ensured that everyone did their chores. Be it collecting the laundry, cleaning the kitchen or chopping logs, there was work to be done in hostels in those days. In my parents' photo album can be found a snapshot of twenty children all stood on stepping stones in the middle of some nearby river, but to this day the abiding memory of the trip was of having to vacuum the sitting room.

These days the YHA has changed. Chores are out, and you don't even need to be a member any more; a simple £3 surcharge providing us with "overnight membership". There were even – gasp – private rooms for two people, one of which we'd secured for the night. We opened it up to find it came fully equipped with ready made beds, fluffy (although rather psychedelically patterned) towels and a kettle with an assorted collection of herbal teas. Quite what that warden from Ilam would have made of it, I don't know, although I'm not entirely sure she would ever have coped.

After settling in, we headed out to see Hawes, making the most of the quiet streets now that the coach parties had moved on to somewhere else. It was a chance to see the sights. And by sights, I really mean "pubs". There were four to choose from, and we wandered up and down the high street peering through the windows to see which tickled our fancy. After discounting two for being too "bog standard", we finally settled on the Crown Inn which turned out to be cosy and friendly, as well as being a purveyor of fine Yorkshire ales, as well as a cracking Barnsley Chop.

More ale followed before, filled up and refreshed, we headed through the dark streets back to the YHA and prepared ourselves for the morning. We had a big day ahead of us, and one which would involve another pub too. And not just any pub, but the highest pub in Britain.

To say I was excited was perhaps an understatement. No, the next day really couldn't come soon enough.

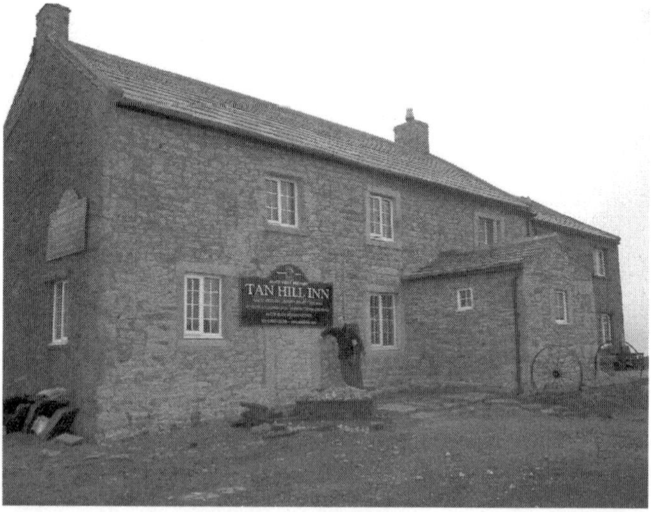
TAN HILL INN

Hawes to Tan Hill Inn

"Well, there's the railway station."

"What railway station? Hawes doesn't have one," replied Catherine, as she peered over the bridge where I was pointing.

"It does. And there's a train at the platform."

It didn't look like it would be leaving the station any time soon though. The little black tank engine, with a set of coaches behind it, didn't really have anywhere to go. The tracks where it sat were long enough to accommodate the train and carriages, and little more. Hawes station hadn't seen a passenger service depart from its platforms since it closed in 1959, and even then, for the last five years of its life there had only been one departure a day in each direction.

Goods services limped on for another five years, but eventually the line between Northallerton and Garsdale was finally closed. The track was lifted, and Hawes's station buildings were left to rot. That was until the 1990s when they were converted to into the new home of the Dales Countryside Museum; at which point the tank engine and coaches were installed.

That said, the little engine may well have to move again one day, at least if plans for the Wensleydale Railway ever come to fruition. The railway has re-opened 22 miles of the old line, and has aspirations to re-open the remaining 18 miles, including Hawes. And if it does, the little black tank engine will have to find a new home. Although, it must be said, that day may be some time away.

* * *

We left the train behind to contemplate its future, and set forth on the Pennine Way once more. The first challenge of the day was a kissing gate, one so narrow that it was almost impossible to pass through with a fully laden rucksack. Even the more svelte Catherine struggled, and I – being a slightly more substantial person – had next to no chance. We fought our way through, cursing whoever thought that this kissing gate was of appropriate design for a popular long distance walking route, and as we did one of the rubber feet from my walking poles pinged off, never to be seen again.

The second task of the day was to get to Hardraw. This was distinctly easier thanks to a relatively flat stroll through fields. It wasn't even that far; just a short distance along the trail, but one which would take us to a pub.

It was a bit early for a pint, but this pub had a special feature in its garden, as a wooden sign on the front of the building made clear. According to it, the pub was owned by D. Mark Thompson, who was an "Innkeeper and Waterfall Provider."

Yes, waterfall provider. For behind the pub is Hardraw Force which is the largest unbroken waterfall in England, at 30m in height. And to see it you have to go through the pub and pay thy toll.

We headed inside to dutifully pay our £2, which – it turned out – had to be given to a distinctly grumpy woman stood in the bar. No sooner had we opened the door and there was a loud and irate "YES?" barked at us. And as for the glare I received as I dared to hand over a £10 note and asked for change...

Later that day we met someone who told us that, because of the state of the service, he did his best to sneak in without paying whenever he could. I couldn't say I blamed him. It was hardly a friendly welcome.

Having escaped from her glaring clutches, we went outside, past the pub's small bandstand, where regular brass band concerts are held, and on via a gentle, peaceful pathway to the waterfall itself. By all accounts it was used as a location in *Robin Hood: Prince of Thieves*; the place where Marion would find Robin bathing underneath. Or so I'm told. The closest I've ever got to seeing that particular Kevin Costner film was when, in 1991 and aged 13, I was accosted in a town centre and persuaded to take part in some market research. This consisted of me watching the film's trailer and answering some mundane questions about it, for absolutely no reward. Still, at least I'd seen the trailer and knew that I really didn't want to watch the film itself.

The waterfall drawn by Alfred Wainwright for inclusion in his Pennine Way book was about twenty times the width of what we saw in front of us. To us it looked like someone had merely shoved a hosepipe at the top, and was water dribble out of it over the rocks. But then when Wainwright did the Pennine Way, it apparently rained pretty much non-stop. Could the two be related? Well, quite possibly.

We left the pub, wondering if the waterfall had been worth the £4 charge, and rejoined the Pennine Way as it went along a walled drovers' path. The path was like a death zone; full, for some reason, of rabbit corpses. And not rabbits that had been caught and partially eaten by some predator. These were just rabbits that seemed to have headed to the path to die, and had then done so. We couldn't walk for more than a few minutes without seeing at least two creatures in various states of decay, and I did wonder why, of all the places they could have gone, they had all chosen this particular lane. Based on the number of corpses, rabbits from miles around had beaten their way here to expire.

In the same way that some people are completely petrified by spiders, I've always been a bit squeamish around dead things. At one time, I'd been known to cross to the other side of the road, if it meant I could avoid having to walk past a dead bird. And whilst in more recent years, my ability to cope with such things has improved, the climb through the graveyard of Hollin Hill was severely trying my recently acquired coping strategies, and it was with much relief that when we stepped out of the walled lane and onto moorland, where the dead animals ceased to be a problem.

*　*　*

We were heading distinctly uphill on a long, gradual climb to the third highest point in Yorkshire, the 716m high Great Shunner Fell.

Some fells have distinct features; a classic outline that can be seen for miles around. But not Shunner Fell which has the kind of shape that suggests someone took a ball of play-dough and flung it on the ground, before sprinkling a load of boulders over the area too, probably as an after thought. There's no steep climb up, and such is the gradualness of the ascent that it takes the Pennine Way 4km in order to climb just 300m in height.

Grey cloud was wrapping itself around the fell and by the time we'd arrived at the stone built shelter at the summit, there was next to nothing to see at all. The cloud had enveloped us almost completely.

"It is as a viewpoint that Great Shunner Fell excels, the panorama being widespread in all directions," says Wainwright, although we saw very little; just a cloak of grey, which we dutifully admired whilst huddling close for warmth in the shelter.

At least there was no chance of us getting lost. Several other fells on the Pennine Way are horrendous to navigate in poor visibility and it's easy to lose your way if you're not careful. On Great Shunner Fell though, it's not a problem. Instead it was a simple task of following the flagstones onwards. And where there weren't flags, there were cairns to lead the way; some of which were taller than myself.

Just as our ascent was slow, so too was our descent as the flags weaved their way through the peat groughs. And as we lost height, so too did we regain visibility and some sense of normality. And then, a mile out of the village of Thwaite, we ended up once more on a walled track that, thankfully, was not lined with the remains of furry creatures. Although if I'd read Wainwright's comment that there's no public toilets in the village "so you had better do it in this lane" before-hand, I may well have thought differently about it all.

Thwaite village itself boasted not one, but two benches and we settled on one of them to rest our legs, and share a packet of cheese and onion crisps before heading on once more.

Our next stop was the village of Keld, just a few miles away and accessed by walking along the side of the small Kisdon Hill, whose height was just enough to give a good view of the villages and the River Swale.

We were now in quintessential Dales farmland; fields lined with dry stone walls, and the Dales's traditional two-level barns. There are hundreds of them dotted around the Dales, and the design is rarely seen anywhere else. Usually built away from the main farm buildings, the barns were designed in such a way that the animals could be housed inside on the ground floor, whilst the feed was kept safely on the first. A foolproof plan, at least until cows learn to climb ladders.

Keld is a perfect place to end a day of walking on the Pennine Way. It has a nice hotel with a friendly bar inside, several welcoming B&Bs and it's at the base of a hill, meaning that you can rest and relax in the evening, and save the hard work for the morning. There's even a tranquil little waterfall, just outside the village, which is perfect spot to sit down and rest if you need to while away some time until the bar opens.

We sat at East Gill Force now, admiring the water crashing gently over the rocks. It was a beautiful spot, enhanced by the autumnal colours of the trees. The kind of place you don't really want to leave. We lingered, and hovered, eking it out as long as we could. But time was pressing on and we needed to get to our accommodation. And alas, that wasn't in Keld, but four miles away up the top of a hill. For whilst Keld may well be a perfect place to spend the night, we were going somewhere even better.

We were staying at the Tan Hill Inn.

These days the Tan Hill Inn sits alone and isolated on the top of Tan Hill. Go back to the seventeenth and eighteenth centuries however and Tan Hill was a hive of activity. This was coal mining territory, and the pub was surrounded by cottages housing the miners and their families. Over the years the mines began to close – the last going in the 1920s – and as a result the pub's fortunes began to fade. At the turn of the twentieth century it spent several years boarded up and derelict, although gained a reprieve with trade coming from mostly from local farmers. The rise of the motorcar also helped develop the pub as a tourist destination, back in the days before drinking and driving became something to be frowned upon. Trade was no doubt also helped in 1954 when Keld's only pub was purchased by a tee-total Methodist preacher who promptly closed it down and converted it into a house; all done in order to save the village from the demons of drink of course. The locals who didn't want to be saved had little choice but to head up the road to the Tan Hill Inn.

The conversion of Keld's former YHA into a hotel means the village is no longer dry, but the idea of spending the night at an isolated pub – and the highest in Britain to boot – was just one we couldn't turn down.

The Tan Hill Inn sits four miles from Keld. Those travelling by car can take the narrow, but steep road up from the village. The Pennine Way instead takes the path over Stonesdale Moor. Waterlogged peat and gushing streams made progress slow, with several large leaps required to cross them. But they were nothing compared to the veritable quagmire of churned up mud caused by diggers and excavators, which were sitting silent and nonchalant; doing their best to persuade passers by that they had not been involved in causing the resulting mayhem at all.

It wasn't exactly clear what work was going on; if it was to improve the path, they seemed to be going about it the wrong way. We even contemplated heading to the sanity of the nearby road instead. Thankfully the disaster zone didn't last long. Beyond the mud, the moorland even began to dry out a little, and the paths clearer and defined. Of the pub though, there seemed to be no sign.

Maps were consulted, and signposts were checked. There was no denying it. We were definitely on the Pennine Way, so it had to be somewhere. More worrying was that the light was beginning to fade, and the last thing we wanted was to be out in the moors in the dark, wandering around trying to find the only building for miles around.

Eventually it was spotted, appearing almost mirage-like out of the gloom; its simple stone building slowly becoming visible in the fading light. And ten minutes later we were stood outside the front door, noting the several cars and even a caravan that were in the small car park.

We gleefully opened the front door and marched towards the bar, only to find ourselves suddenly stopped in our tracks by the sight of a duck sat in an old iron bathtub in front of the pub's roaring fire. Next to it lay a dog, dozing in the light of the flames.

The dog, it turned out, was called Sherbert, and the duck was a victim of decades of intensive breeding. Which given it was only four months old, was quite an achievement. We were filled in on the detail by the pub's landlady. Over many, many years, ducks have been selectively bred to gain weight fast; the fatter the duck, the better the price the farmer would get for it. Unfortunately this means that some ducks grow so fast that their legs can't support the weight of the body. In other words, it can't stand up, and do all the exciting things that a duck's life usually involves. The duck needed an intensive course of physiotherapy and that's exactly what it was now being provided with, starting with a course of aqua-aerobics in the tin bath.

The duck's battles with health duly noted, we headed to our rooms to refresh before returning to the bar for the serious business of the day: sampling the Tan Hill Inn's wares.

For walkers who set off from Keld in the morning, the Tan Hill Inn comes at a slightly annoying time. Leave Keld at 9am and you'll reach the top of Tan Hill around 11. Too early for lunch, and certainly too early for a pint, meaning the visiting walker will end up nursing a cup of coffee with a glum look on their face. Such a walker has come inside, seen what they could have been enjoying, and begun to regret the way they organised their itinerary. Even having never been to the Tan Hill Inn before, we'd known that organising our trip that way would be fundamentally flawed.

In contrast, our approach meant that whilst we'd had an unwelcome slog up hill at the end of the day, we did have a full evening to sample the pub's fine range of ales. And this we did, pulling up a stool at the bar from where we could soak in the Tan Hill's atmosphere, and prepared ourselves for fully loaded plates groaning with the pub's fine home-cooking.

"Do you fancy a Chinese?" asked the man behind the bar. "We're getting a take-away."

We paused, looked at each other and wondered if we'd suddenly got transported into a different universe. One where the pub wasn't sat on isolated moorland, but instead was sat in an urban metropolis with "The Golden Palace" takeaway next door. We looked outside the window, but it clearly wasn't. Given the nearest village didn't even have a shop, the nearest takeaway must have been some way away.

Maybe if we'd been walking the Pennine Way all in one go, we would have taken them up on the offer. On longer walking trips, night after night of pub grub can get a bit tiresome. You begin to long for something different; something other than yet another steak and ale pie, or fish and chips. As it was, we'd been walking for a mere two days. And the Tan Hill Inn's menu included a giant Yorkshire Pudding, filled with mash, sausages and gravy. There was just no competition, and I knew I'd made the right choice.

As the night went on, the pub felt snugger and snugger. The staff treated everyone as if they were old friends, even if they had just turned up a few hours earlier with soggy boots. Here, in the middle of nowhere, every customer was a local. And when I finished my pint whilst the staff were still wolfing down their sweet and sour chicken with egg fried rice, I couldn't have been happier to hear the words "Pop round and serve yourself!"

Grasping the handpull, I executed the delivery of a near perfect pint of Theakston's Old Perculier; my first pint poured since my last shift behind the university bar some eight years earlier.

"I think I like this place," I said to Catherine as I returned to the rightful side of the bar.

"Me too," she replied.

I knew for sure, this place was going to be hard to beat.

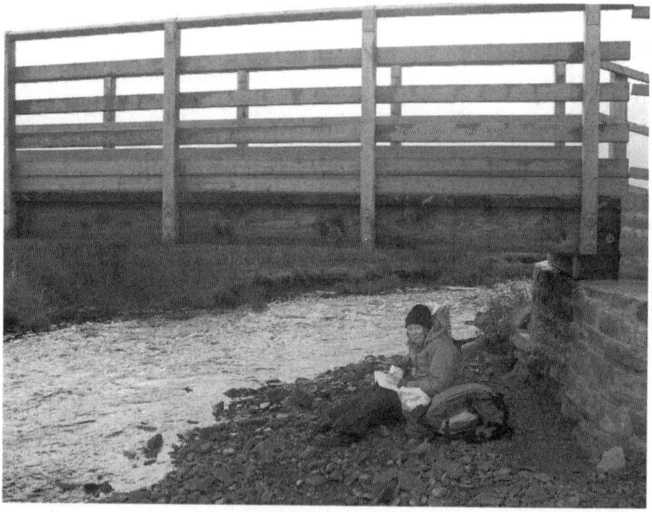

Tan Hill Inn to Middleton-in-Teesdale

In all my life I can't think of a pub I've loved quite as much as the Red Lion in Ealing, West London. A relatively small pub, it served great beers, wonderful food and its walls were decorated with film memorabilia relating to Ealing Studios which were across the road.

It also had a fantastic walled beer garden, where every year birds would nest. In late spring, young chicks would be seen hopping around between tables. Yes, the Red Lion was special all right. I loved visiting it, and it was the first pub where I was considered to be a "regular"; a badge I wore with pride.

After four years we moved out of Ealing; forced to move by property prices. We were looking to buy a house, and Ealing was just too expensive. A two bedroom flat would have cost us at least three times the amount we eventually spent on our new home in south west London; money we simply didn't have.

A few days before we moved, we paid one final visit to the Red Lion. Saying goodbye was a real wrench. I didn't want to go. Catherine almost had to drag me out of the building.

No pub has ever been so difficult to leave, although frankly, the Tan Hill Inn was certainly giving it a run for its money. One night there and I was smitten. If I lived nearby, I would have been hooked for life. Although as there were no houses nearby, I'm not entirely sure where I would be living for that to ever happen.

The weather was also doing its best to persuade us to stay. I'd been woken up at 6am by the sound of heavy rain, and whilst it had stopped by the time we'd finished breakfast and paid our bill, the cloud was low and visibility poor.

Being able to see where you're going is actually quite important when leaving the Tan Hill Inn. The Pennine Way follows a path along Sleightholme Moor, however in bad weather, it can be a dangerous place and therefore an alternative route exists by following the road. The decision on which to take needs to be taken pretty much at the pub door.

"Which way are you going then?" asked a fellow walker, who we'd been chatting to over breakfast.

"Probably the main route," replied Catherine who had taken charge of navigation for the day.

Eyebrows were raised; glances at the weather made. A long pause followed.

"I think we're going down the road. We're doing a half day to Bowes. Need to get some laundry done. Have a good walk!" And with that she wandered off along the deserted tarmac with her husband. She might even have been shaking her head.

I looked at Catherine, and Catherine looked back, and we both stared at the weather.

"We can always turn back if it's bad," I said.

"Yeah," she replied, with a tone that suggested that there was no way that was going to happen.

As it turned out, Tan Hill's bark was worse than its bite. The cloud loosened up a bit as we lost a little height, and the path was just visible enough to ensure we wouldn't lose it. By 10am, the sun had even come out for a short while, and we were treated to some lovely sights as the bright light hit the mossy ground. In fact the biggest challenge was fording the many streams that filled the moor, and the word "ford" appears frequently as the Pennine Way traverses it. There was so many that the Ordnance Survey might as well just have written "FORD" in big letters over the whole area and saved themselves a lot of hassle.

* * *

At Trough Heads farm, the Pennine Way walker needs to make a decision. Or, realistically, needs to act upon a decision made some months earlier whilst drawing up an itinerary and booking accommodation. Whatever. It's still a decision that needs to be made. And it's one that goes like this: do I go to Bowes or not?

After leaving the Tan Hill Inn, the Pennine Way doesn't pass any towns or villages for sixteen miles until it arrives in Middleton-in-Teesdale. In contrast, Bowes is a mere nine miles from the Tan Hill Inn.

There's a snag. To get to Bowes requires a two and a half mile detour off the Pennine Way. Which is why the Bowes Loop was created. It's an alternative route that heads east from the farm to the village, and then meanders north in order to re-meet the main route near Blackton Reservoir. It's a little longer, but means walkers don't have to double back on themselves.

For those that set off from Keld and who don't fancy a twenty mile day to Middleton, the Bowes Loop is an appealing option – as it is if you urgently need to clean some clothes. For us though, it was a bit pointless, and we'd decided to go the whole hog and press on. Besides, it meant we could pass over "God's Bridge" and a dismantled railway. And let's be honest, who wouldn't choose that option over the romantic ruins of Bowes castle and an early afternoon pint?

God's Bridge turned out to be a large slab of limestone, which forms a natural crossing over the River Greta. And the dismantled railway, well that was like most dismantled railways; in this case part of the line that once ran between Kirkby Stephen and Bishop Auckland that was inevitably closed down by that arch-villain of Britain's railway network, Doctor Richard Beeching.

Whilst the fact that the railway went through a sparsely populated area with little traffic did contribute to its demise, the rise of the motor vehicle helped hammer the nail into the coffin. Roads stole much of the railway's traffic as the local population obtained cars, and freight moved to lorries. Today the railway has been replaced by the A66 dual carriageway, under which the Pennine

Way travels in a specially constructed subway.

Footpaths under roads are rarely nice things to go under; usually dark and dank with deep puddles of water waiting to surprise anyone daring to set foot in the tunnel. The designers of this subway had thought about this carefully and had come up with a solution. They'd installed light switches at each end of the tunnel. Unfortunately though, the switches did nothing. No matter how much we pressed them, there was no illumination at all. Thankfully there wasn't a dead sheep waiting for us to trip over. Just some muddy puddles instead.

Out in the air again, the green (and slightly muddy) fields were replaced by moorland; a wide track leading us along past clumps of heather and wild grasses. It was nearly lunchtime and we were eagerly watching out for somewhere to stop for some food, however what few places there were, would do little bar provide us with soggy bottoms. And then, after a few miles of walking, we struck gold next to a stream, which the Pennine Way crossed on a bridge. There were walls to shelter from the wind behind, and there were large boulders to sit on. An ideal picnic spot. We looked at each other, sat down and got out our sandwiches.

Ten seconds later, it began to rain.

Faced with eating our food in the rain, or keep on waking in the no doubt vain hope that there would be a nice, sheltered alternative in the next hour or so, we did the only thing you could do in such circumstances. We put on our waterproofs and huddled under the bridge.

As Catherine noted dryly, "You haven't done the Pennine Way properly if you haven't had to eat lunch huddled under a bridge."

* * *

Blackton Reservoir roughly marks the half-way point for the Pennine Way. Which meant there was only a mere 130 miles to Kirk Yetholm then. There was no official marker for this moment, although some thoughtful person had scrawled "half way, losers!" on a stile.

The reservoir was mostly surrounded by fields grazed by sheep, but one contained a wildlife reserve named Hannah's Meadow. The land was once owned by Hannah Hauxwell, who came to prominence in the 1972 Yorkshire Television programme, 'Too Long a Winter'. The documentary chronicled the difficult conditions endured by the farmers of the north Pennines, with some focus on Hannah who lived by herself in a dilapidated farmhouse with no electricity or running water. Her few cattle brought her in a meagre income of £250 a year at a time when the average salary cane in at £2,000.

It's perhaps a cliché to say it, but Hannah's story touched a nation. For days after broadcast, viewers bombarded Yorkshire Television's phone lines in an attempt to find out how they could help and enough money was raised to help improve conditions by connecting the farm to the National Grid.

The programme may have put Hannah in the public eye, and improved her life a little, but she continued at the farm for another 16 years until she decided to retire. The farm itself was purchased by the Durham Wildlife Trust who were attracted to its potential as a nature reserve thanks to the fact that in her fifty years there, Hannah had only ever used traditional farming practices, and had never used artificial fertilisers. In short, it was something special.

Today, the Trust maintains that style of farming, with the result that the land retains a rich and diverse range of wildlife that has been lost from more intensively farmed land in the area. Visit in the summer and you'll find a range of traditional wild-meadow flowers. Come in October like we did, and you probably just find a rather plain field. Such is the way, sometimes.

The lush greenery around the reservoir was short-lived, and it wasn't long before we had returned to moorland. Even the sky seemed to reflect the change. When we'd been passing Blackton it looked like the sun might try and burst through, but a mile later the clouds had gone dark and brooding. Could the weather really be watching what we were up to, and changing accordingly? Unlikely perhaps, but it was one hell of a coincidence.

We were heading towards another set of reservoirs at Grassholme, and I did wonder if the weather would suddenly change again when we got there. And indeed it did, with a little patch of blue appearing. Not much, but enough to cheer our hearts a little. The sheep at How Farm were another matter entirely.

A large group had been collected into a smallish field near some farm buildings; a field that naturally the Pennine Way had to cross directly. No sooner had we entered it and the sheep started stampeding towards us, anxious to say hello. We walked through as quickly as possible, desperate to shake them off and by the time we had reached the end of the field, they'd almost caught up with us, and we were pretty much running; rushing to scramble over the stile and into the next field. Safe, secure and exhausted, we climbed over on the other side, and headed – without any sheep – to the edge of Grassholme Reservoir where there was a conveniently sited bench to sit on for a while whilst we caught our breath. And boy did we need to.

Our path continued to snake its way along more fields; the sheep now kept firmly at bay by drystone walls. We were now just a few miles away from Middleton-in-Teesdale, the buildings of which slowly came into view as we made away over the moorland. Soon we were wandering round the town's streets, attempting to find our B&B which proved to be completely impossible despite it having a large sign and a highly prominent location on the high street.

Despite being completely covered in mud, we were warmly welcomed by the B&B's owner and promptly shown to our room, and plied with hot tea and homemade biscuits. Belvedere House swiftly found itself filed under the "luxury" accommodation category, which always made us feel extra guilty about filling our room up with soggy waterproofs, and mud-strewn trousers. Everything in the place looked extremely well presented; simple, comfortable elegance, and for good measure it proved to be one of the cheaper places we stayed on the entire trip. When we came to write our "top places on the Pennine Way" guide, this place was going to get a raving review.

Having dutifully sprayed the room's recently painted walls with muck and murk, and covered the floor with our belongings, it was time to go out and see what Middleton-in-Teesdale had to offer. The streets were lined with a number of small, independent businesses, but seemed rather short on anywhere to get an evening meal. There was a pub next to our B&B but it seemed to be in darkness; whether permanently or temporarily, we couldn't tell. Another on the entrance to Middleton had a sign saying "No food" so that was out. This just left a chippy, and the rather large hotel, which dominated the high street.

The hotel's small bar was heaving; full of people sitting on the 1970s style lounge furniture, all upholstered in pink velour. Although in some respects it felt more like a doctor's waiting room than somewhere to relax and unwind. Almost everyone there was waiting for a meal, and every time a member of staff entered, twenty-odd heads turned to see if it was their time to adjourn to the dining area.

We perched at the bar – all the pink armchairs being taken – and began to feel we really should be wearing something smarter than our walking trousers and fleeces, and perhaps drinking something more sophisticated than a pint of real ale. A cocktail perhaps?

Finally, our names were called, and the young waitress led us down a short corridor to the dining room, and our table. Within minutes a full canteen worth of cutlery had been deposited in front of us, with silver salt and pepper pots added for good measure; the staff obviously having the expectation that we were about to partake in five courses of fine dining. Although this didn't particularly seem to go with the menu for the evening.

Like most of the places we ate at on the Pennine Way, the hotel seemed to offer a pretty standard Pennine Way "pub grub" menu. Occasionally we'd find ourselves in a place where the menu was a bit more creative, but nine times out of ten it would be a variation on a familiar theme. Garlic mushrooms, prawn cocktail and pate and toast would invariably feature on the starters section, whilst the main courses would always include gammon and pineapple, steak, a lamb shank and scampi and chips. Vegetarians would, without fail, have a choice of vegetable lasagne or mushroom stroganoff, and pretty much everything would come with a choice of potatoes and boiled vegetables.

Generally the menus gave the impression they hadn't changed for decades. "Modern" cuisine such as burgers were rarely featured, and even if a curry had somehow managed to sneak onto the menu, there'd be a high probability that it would be "beef", and be served with chips and salad.

All this is not to say that the food was bad. Generally the food we ate on the Pennine Way was perfectly fine. Sometimes it was fantastic. But the one thing it wasn't was varied. In the context of a bustling rural pub though, it all seemed to work. But when surrounded by a table groaning under the weight of silverware in an enormous yet silent hotel dining room, it just seemed bizarre, and it was almost a relief to get out of the place and head on our way.

Now that it was empty of diners, the hotel's bar felt more like a place to relax than wait, however we were in little mood for a late night. We'd had a long day, and the next would be even longer. We had twenty miles to do in order to reach Dufton and we'd need to get an early start if we were to reach there before the sun set. It was definitely time for bed.

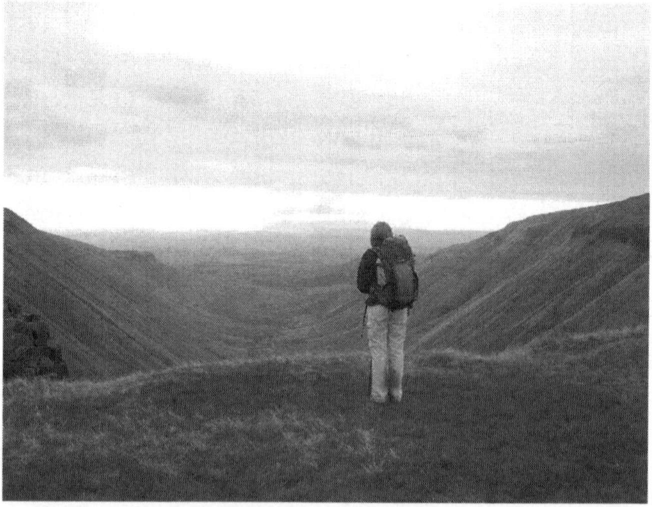

Middleton-in-Teesdale to Dufton

Whatever way you cut up the Pennine Way, chances are you're going to end up with a monster of a day of walking at some point. Indeed, the very first day on the trail – heading out of Edale – is a compulsory 16 mile hike, whereas the last section from Byrness to Kirk Yetholm comes in at 25 miles, unless you can cadge a lift or are prepared to take an epic detour in order to reach some overnight accommodation.

For us, the walk to Dufton would be one of those walks. Twenty miles to do, and with a time limit. We simply had to get there before the last vestiges of sunlight disappeared at 6pm. Such is the joy of walking in October.

It need not have been thus. It's perfectly possible to split the section up by taking a break at the village of Langdon Beck, which boasts a youth hostel and pub, and is just a short way off the trail. But almost inevitably we were up against the clock. We needed to race back to London the following day, and that meant we needed to finish reasonably close to a railway station. True, Dufton wasn't exactly close to one, but a taxi would be able to take us to Penrith in roughly twenty minutes. So a long walk it was then and after an early breakfast from our obliging B&B landlady, we hit the road.

Most of the day would be spent with a watery

accompaniment, as the Pennine Way followed the River Tees upstream towards its source. The river, which flows for eighty-five miles to the North Sea near Middlesborough, starts its journey on the slopes of Cross Fell.

For the first two miles or so out of Middleton-in-Teesdale, the path stayed a respectful distance away from the river, heading across fields instead, before finally joining a riverside path near a stretch of woodland. We wandered along happily, enjoying the opportunity to sample some non-moorland scenery. Large trees grew on both sides, giving the river a tranquil feel, despite its best efforts to crash noisily over rocks. The Tees seemed to be a river in a hurry; there was no time for it to relax. It just had to get to the sea, and clearly as fast as possible.

There were few places where this was more apparent than Low Force waterfall where the water plunges down a five and a half metre drop. There was even a chance to get a cracking view of the water courtesy of Wynch Bridge, a narrow suspension bridge which was first opened in 1830. A sign warned that only one person should try crossing the bridge at any time, and woe betide any large groups that tried to all go on at the same time as the county council certainly wouldn't be held responsible for whatever madness then ensured. The bridge certainly swayed badly enough with just one of us on it, and I dreaded to think how it might be if more tried to cross at the same time.

Low Force was but a mere warm up to what was further upstream. High Force is a far bigger waterfall, with the water plunging down 21m. And whilst its height may be less than that of Hardraw Force which we'd seen a few days earlier, High Force certainly packs its punch with sheer impact. The water crashes and thunders down, spraying enthusiastically as it reaches the bottom, and can get on its way.

High Force certainly knew how to put on a show, and we sat down at a convenient vantage point with a biscuit in hand, and watched it do what it did best. On the other side of the river it's possible to drive up, park your car – for a fee – and wander to a viewing area to see the waterfall and as we sat a couple did just that. But their reward for doing so was merely to see the waterfall from the bottom, looking up. From where we were, I had no doubt that the best view was on our side of the river. With no road access, those on foot had, without doubt, been rewarded for their efforts.

* * *

Beyond High Force, the Pennine Way headed away from the river; as if it felt that the waterfall simply couldn't be beat, and that walkers had better be taken away from it as quickly as possible so that they could look at something else, and so not be disappointed.

That something else were the whitewashed buildings, which were dotted around the valley below; each house and building being required to be painted that way as part of the lease agreement with the Raby Estate, which owns much of the area. The story goes that one day, one of the many Lord Barnards from history was out hunting and became stranded in a storm. He headed to a farmhouse, believing it to be one of his own properties, but he was mistaken and despite the bitter weather, was refused shelter. Determined that he would never make the same mistake again, he insisted that from thenceforth any building on his estate must be painted white. A rather extreme reaction perhaps, but then just what is the point in being a rich landowner if you can't set an absurd rule or two?

Our separation from the Tees was short lived, and we were rejoined with it once more, initially through fields and meadows, but soon hoping between rocky boulders in a narrow passage between the river and the side of a hill. And then it was time to head uphill slightly, on a rocky path that spent a lot of time being unnervingly close to the gushing waterfall of Cauldron Snout.

True, it wasn't a case of climbing up a waterfall. Thankfully. But there's just something about rocky paths going uphill next to copious amounts of water that makes me insanely nervous. Something to do with me being a rather large and slightly clumsy chap with big feet and a tendency to lose my balance at the touch of a hat probably. This is then compounded by carrying a large rucksack, which distorts the body's centre of mass, and when I do feel I'm liable to fall over, I'm not even entirely sure which direction I should be leaning in order to save the day. Add water into the mix, and suddenly visions of mountain rescue and air ambulances start filling my mind. The same thing happens every time I see a fell runner. How do they do it, I wonder, as they leap nimbly from rock to rock as they descend some insanely steep, scree-filled slope? If I tried that, I'd end up at the bottom very quickly that's for sure, and it probably wouldn't be all in one piece.

Reading this, you may begin to think that this was some epic, dangerous climb; that life and limb were being threatened as we attempted to get to the top of the waterfall. It would make a good tale, no doubt. Unfortunately for lovers of excitement and drama – or indeed, people who are reading this desperately hoping that mountain rescue and the North East Air Ambulance will feature – it didn't happen. The climb wasn't that big as Cauldron Snout comes in at a mere 60m in height, although the gradient of the waterfall is so shallow that its actual length comes in at 180m long. And for that effort, what's the reward? Well a view of a dam; specifically the dam at the head of Cow Green Reservoir, which holds back a whopping 40,000 million litres of water. It's big all right.

We crossed the Tees on a bridge in the shadow of the dam, and said our final farewells to the river. It was also time for a change in the Pennine Way. The sheep began to disappear, to be replaced by the remains of an old mine, and then by red flags.

For here the Pennine Way passes over moorland that is part of the North Pennines Area of Outstanding Natural Beauty, the North Pennine

Moors Special Protection Area, and Moorhouse and Upper Teesdale Special Area of Conservation. And it's also regularly used by the military to blast the living bejeebers out of everything. The army have been using Warcop Training Area to practice driving tanks since 1942, and show no sign of leaving. There are public rights of way across some of it, although they're not much use to anyone unless you want to use them after 1pm on a Sunday. The army apparently use the training area most of the week, although do sometimes have an occasional day off; one of which seemed to coincide with our visit.

Accessing the Pennine Way is, of course, never a problem. It passes along the north of the range and the only sign that this is not "normal" country is the row of red flags and warning signs that dot the landscape. Oh and the huge scars on the hillside caused by the tanks that regularly roam the area.

It's a rather grim sight; disheartening and dispiriting. Was this really the best place for them to practise driving tanks? It was a relief to finally traverse the couple of miles along the training area border, and come alongside the flowing water of Maize Beck. It gave us something to look at that wasn't long straight rows of churned mud.

On the other hand, with little to see and enjoy, we could simply get our heads down and push on. There were many miles still to do. And anyway, there was something special coming our way. Something very special.

And that was High Cup Nick.

There are many stunning sights on the Pennine Way; natural and man made. Ribblehead Viaduct, the limestone pavement at Malham Cove, the Tan Hill Inn looming out of the cloud, and of course the splendour of Kinder Scout. Yet arguably High Cup is on another level.

There's an element of expectation for some time as you get closer and closer. You can see something is about to happen; little hints that there's something ahead although you're not really sure what. Further on you walk, getting closer and closer to main view point, until suddenly all is revealed. In front of you is a massive U shaped valley, looking for all intents and purposes like a giant had scooped out a massive chunk of the hillside, leaving a huge crater behind. It's awesome, it's splendid and it's utterly stunning. There was no denying it, this was something amazing. Even the fact that in order to see it, I'd tripped up and fallen in a stream I was trying to ford, couldn't stifle my enthusiasm for the place.

We stood there just looking, in silence and in awe. Constantly looking. Behind us a herd of wild horses frolicked and played, but who cared. This was the money shot; the highlight of the whole day. And, besides the horses, we had the place to ourselves. For High Cup is off the beaten track; three miles away from the nearest road which means that anyone who comes to see it has to do so under their own steam. Were there a car park nearby, High Cup would no doubt be full of people. Probably even a café and a small gift shop; and no doubt some visitors wandering up with moaning comments such as "is that it?" before whipping out their smartphone to complain about it on TripAdvisor.

But for those on foot, High Cup is a fantastic reward for the effort. I could have spent hours there, just staring. And would have done, had it not been for one tiny issue.

"It's quarter to five," I said, looking at my watch.

"Oh," Catherine replied sadly.

We had another three or so miles to do, and seventy five minutes in which to do them in before the light faded. We hadn't spent anywhere near enough time at High Cup, but we really couldn't spend much more.

At least the Pennine Way heads along the north side of High Cup, meaning we could eke it out a little longer, but eventually we just had to bid it farewell and push on to Dufton.

As we headed downhill to the Eden Valley, the sky began to change. The weather had been pretty gloomy all day, however now the sky was preparing itself for a show, and it looked like it was going to be special. The sun shone brightly under the cloud, casting a bright glow over all the area, providing a sense of drama when coupled with the black clouds.

Then as it got lower and lower, the whole area began to be bathed in pink, then gold, and we prepared ourselves for one of the finest sunsets we'd ever seen. Two special treats in one day? The Pennine Way was spoiling us.

It was all over by the time we arrived on the road

that would take us the quarter of a mile into Dufton, and as we arrived outside the village's youth hostel, the light had pretty much gone. We were completely exhausted. My back was aching, and Catherine's knee was playing up, and both of us were completely footsore after our twenty mile walk.

After collapsing on our beds, we finally managed to raise enough energy to head to pub; staggering across the dark village green like zombies to the warm, welcoming embrace of the Stag Inn in order to sup a few pints, purely for medicinal reasons naturally. Sitting in the cosy bar area in front of the pub's warm and welcoming fire, we quietly eavesdropped onto the conversations of some locals who were conversing about the latest news about the local Women's Institute branch, which had decided to disband and reform in a different form. We never did get to the bottom of why that happened, but we were too tired to really care.

Later I headed to the pub's toilets. In the gents I spied an old, faded photograph of a group of people from decades gone by, sat down at the head of High Cup. I stared at it, nodded to myself, and headed back to the bar. There was a long train journey home the next day, but there was time for one last pint, I was sure.

Part 4

Dufton to Byrness
Fourth trip walking the Pennine Way

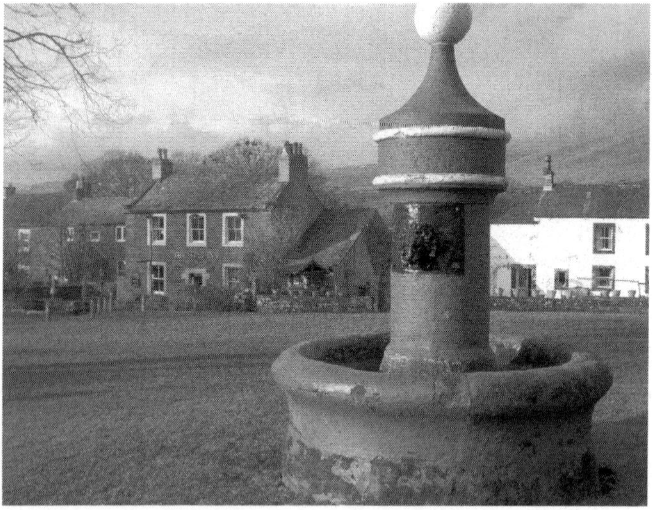

Dufton to Garrigill

Even on a cold and rather dull morning in March, Dufton was a hard place not to like. What is there not to love about clusters of houses and cottages neatly arranged around the village green, with a red circular fountain and water trough taking pride of place in the middle, and all overlooked by the 481m high Dufton Pike?

It ticked all the boxes. Beautiful location? Check. Fantastic village pub? Check. Conveniently sited youth hostel, able to accommodate lots of people for those times when you hold an absolutely huge party in your new house? Check. Looks great even in dismal weather? Check. Excellent public transport services and a shop selling milk that you can pop out to when you've run out of the stuff?

Err... Hang on...

Well you can't have everything, can you?

We'd arrived at Dufton the previous evening, two and a half years after our last visit. We'd even been given the same room in the youth hostel. The Stag Inn seemed a little quieter, although on the other hand there was someone smoking the place out by putting their soggy boots in one of the compartments of the large cast iron range that dominated the pub's main room.

A sign in the bar promoted the pub's annual Easter events, including an egg hunt, a "Chicken

Race" (please bring your own chicken) and even a delayed "New Years Day" Buggy Race, If only we'd been there a week later.

To make the whole visit even more idyllic, over breakfast the next morning we were treated to the view of a red squirrel taking nuts from the YHA's back garden. Did we really have to leave this place? Well yes we did. We were back in Dufton for a reason. We were about to finish the Pennine Way. In eight days time we'd be in the Border Inn in Kirk Yetholm, raising a celebratory pint having finally done the whole thing. This was what we'd been working towards for the past three years.

What's more, our final stretch of the Pennine Way would involve the mighty Cheviots, Hadrian's Wall, a stay in a remote farm and would all start off with a climb up the highest point on the whole trail. Yes it was a wrench to leave Dufton, but there was so much to look forward to.

* * *

Although there's been a settlement at Dufton since ancient times, the village that's there now owes much of its existence to lead mining. Several mines nearby were opened in the 18th century by The London Lead Company, which, despite its name, was based in Middleton-in-Teesdale. The Quaker owned company built most of the current cottages, industrial buildings and even a water supply system.

Even the route by which the Pennine Way left

the village had a mining link, following a lane once used by miners on their way to the small mines on the fells ahead. Of course, the mines are all gone now. The bottom fell out of the lead market in the closing years of the 19th century, and soon most of the mines had closed, leaving many a household without employment, and requiring Dufton to find a new role in life, which it did in farming and tourism.

"There's a sheep stuck in that ditch over there," cried Catherine, pointing at said creature in the field adjoining the track, which was bleating forlornly. "They can't get up if they're stuck on their back," she added. "We'd better help it. Who knows when the farmer might spot it."

Before I knew it, she was marching across the field determined to rescue a sheep in distress. This proved easier said than done. The sight of a human with a large red rucksack on her back was more than enough to send the animal into even more of a tizz and panic. With a heaving and a lot of grunting – and a fair amount of fighting back – we somehow managed to turn the sheep the right way up, and let it run off before we checked ourselves for damage, which mainly consisted of a heavy coating of mud from the churned up field. Oh well, chances were we would be getting muddy anyway.

Dusting ourselves down, we returned the path, heading past an abandoned farmhouse – complete with a rusting, abandoned tractor – and we began the climb that would eventually take us to Cross Fell.

As we began to rise, we looked back at the land we were leaving behind. Dufton sits nestling in the Eden Valley; a lush green and attractive looking place; the sun peering down over it, through some cracks in the clouds. On a good day, even the Lake District is visible. Ah, lovely.

And then there was where we were going. Dull, rocky, grey, hard, gloomy. It was hard not to think that we were going in the wrong direction.

Even in great weather, there's a high chance of cloud covering the top of Cross Fell and its neighbours. And whilst the conditions weren't terrible for us, they certainly weren't brilliant by any means, and we quickly found ourselves walking through dense cloud trying to work out exactly where the path was going. This was a task that was made even harder when we reached a large section that was under a blanket of snow. Rather naively, snow was the one thing that we hadn't planned for on the trip; the idea that there may still be some on these cold, windswept fells at the end of March, simply not having crossed our minds.

Given we'd both grown up with the edges of the Pennines on our doorsteps, we probably should have known better, however ten years living in London where snow is rare and barely lasts a day or two when it does fall, had perhaps made us complacent. There was obviously going to be some snow up in the hills at the end of March. Oh well. We'd remember next time.

A trail of footprints in the snow suggested the route to follow, and after cross-checking with the map, it seemed like they were going the way we needed to go. And thankfully the snow was relatively short-lived, and our ascent to the giant cairn at the summit of Knock Fell – the first of several fell tops we'd reach on our way up to Cross Fell – continued without too much further incident.

The path to neighbouring Great Dun Fell was less clear. The fell is covered in cloud two thirds of the year; it's so prevalent that for many years the University of Manchester had a meteorological station here, in order to study clouds. Naturally on a cold, gloomy March morning, the chances of us seeing anything at all were pretty slim, and the fog grew thicker and thicker just at a time when the path was getting more and more indistinct.

Progress was slow as compasses were regularly consulted, and maps checked against what little scenery was visible. Every time some validation that we were indeed on the correct path was obtained, was followed by a small celebration; the most obvious being a tarmacked road, which lead to the fell's summit. Most of the road was covered by heavy snow, with the only sign that it existed being the row of tall poles lining the edge of it, for use in aiding cars in just such circumstances. Tyre marks suggested the poles had been useful for someone recently too.

The summit of Great Dun Fell is home to an air traffic control radar station, including a dome structure, and a couple of large transmitters that slowly began to loom out of the cloud as we got closer to the top. Fences around the complex prevented us from getting a good view of any of it; the cloud making visibility so low that we could still barely see the large dome building even when stood at the perimeter fence just a few metres away.

With little incentive to stick around, we pushed on the short distance to the summit of Little Dun Fell, which, despite its name, is only a mere 8m shorter than its neighbour. Its summit cairn was suitably small as well with the top marked by a tiny pile of rocks, giving the impression that the local cairn builders simply couldn't have been bothered by it.

The top also housed a small stone shelter, and we took the chance to escape from the bitter winds, and have some food; our feet resting on a small pile of snow that had somehow managed to survive whilst the rest that had fallen on the fell had long melted.

Our guide book told us that the view from Little Dun Fell was disappointing. Well of that there was no doubt; we couldn't see anything at all. But, the book went on, it was all made up by the "prospect of Cross Fell which now takes on Goliath proportions." We had to take its word for it.

If you thought the chances of getting a cloud free summit at Little Dun Fell were low, the situation at Cross Fell is even worse. It's rarely out of cloud, and it's not unheard of for the winter snow to remain on top until July; there's even been reports of fresh snow appearing in June. All this on a fell top where the path is nearly invisible, resulting in a tricky navigational challenge.

Using Catherine's patented technique of checking the map and compass every two minutes though, the chances of us getting significantly lost were pretty low and we made it to the summit without any major complications. With it came a double celebration, for Cross Fell is not just any old fell. Standing at 893m above sea level, we'd reached the highest point of the whole of the Pennine Way. As if to celebrate, a small crack formed in the cloud, revealing a patch of blue underneath.

We'd done well indeed.

* * *

After spending the morning walking through dense cloud, it took some adjusting to being back in normal conditions again. The cloud began to part almost as soon as we began to descend from Cross Fell and navigation also got easier as we joined a rough track that led us to Greg's Hut.

Originally a cottage built to support the local lead mines, it was abandoned after the mines closed and may have remained so were it not for the sad death of John Gregory in a climbing accident in the Alps in 1968. A group of his friends got together and adopted the hut, and renovated it in his memory, opening it up as a bothy and naming it Greg's Hut. To this day the Greg's Hut Association continue to maintain what is the highest bothy in England; possibly the highest in the whole of the UK.

We popped inside for some shelter, joining the 600 or so other visitors recorded in the bothy log book, before heading on our way, passing by old mine workings and spoil heaps. The sun made a brief appearance, and looking behind us revealed that the cloud had now lifted from Great Dun Fell, giving us a clearer view of the radar station than we'd had when we were stood right next to it. We had looked back at just the right point too; a little further on and the fell would be completely hidden from our path.

Several miles of moorland were now ahead of us, covered with patches of snow at regular intervals. We were once again following an old miners track, and it was hard not to think of the long journey the miners had from their homes in the valleys, and the hard life they lived. The stone path was certainly hard enough on our feet, cushioned as they were by modern boot technology. Walking in clogs over these moors on a weekly basis, must have been quite a trek.

Remnants of the mines could be seen dotted all over the place; old workings, occasional huts and spoil heaps all present. Another remnant was under our feet. Small purple stones were regularly dotted over the track, part of the waste of the old mines. The stones contain fluorspar. When dry they appear clear and opaque, but give them a good dose of water and they glow their mysterious, yet attractive colour.

It took almost eight miles from the top of Cross Fell, but eventually we arrived at the welcoming sight of Garrigill, meaning our day was ending.

There was a depressing sight to greet us at the village green however. There'd be no welcoming pint of ale to celebrate a long day's walking; the village pub was empty and boarded up. Its closure hadn't been a surprise to us; we'd been warned by the owner of our B&B when we booked, and had arranged to eat an evening meal in our B&B instead. We'd even had to break the news of the pub's closure to the warden at Dufton Youth Hostel who had, on hearing we were heading to Garrigill, told us it was a "cracking pub." The boards would come off and the pub would re-open again nine months later, but even that would be relatively short-lived.

It just felt wrong not to be supping a pint of ale in the evening. Walking holidays in Britain have often been equated to a multi-day pub crawl, and it's rare on the Pennine Way that you couldn't end the day with a pint in your hand. But alas, Garrigill's nearest pub now lay three miles away in Alston; far too far away for these two weary Pennine Way walkers to reach.

Pubs are the beating heart of most communities in Britain, and Garrigill felt like it had something ripped out of it. There was little else to do, so we spent most of the evening in our room at the B&B watching TV and feeling rather cooped up and just ever so listless.

We resolved however to make up for it the next day, for then we'd be passing through the town of Alston. And with just nine miles to walk, we'd have plenty of time to check out the sights, and, of course, a good lunch. Perhaps in a pub, with a pint or two. Frankly, it was the least we could do.

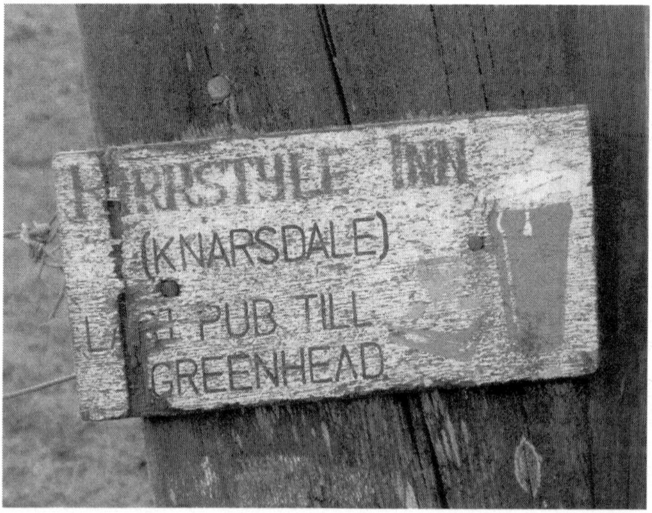
(KNARSDALE)
PUB TILL
GREENHEAD

Garrigill to Slaggyford

For many Pennine Way walkers, the trip from Dufton is a twenty mile epic, arriving at the bustling market town of Alston. This is then followed by a further sixteen and a half miles the next day in order to reach Greenhead.

Such an itinerary means that the walker arrives at Garrigill, sees a lovely village with its welcoming B&Bs, and can do nothing but sigh as they're forced to plod on for another four miles. They have no choice. Their itinerary demands it. Their accommodation is waiting up the road. Although, it must be said, maybe the sight of a boarded up pub might hurry their progress on a little.

There is, however, another way, by breaking at Garrigill and then stopping somewhere between Alston and Greenhead for a second night. It's not straightforward thanks to the dearth of places to stay, but do your research and you may find one of those rare places in the Knarsdale area.

And that's exactly what we planned to do. We had our bed booked at a small (and now, I'm afraid to say, closed) B&B at Slaggyford, a mile or so before Knarsdale, and had a leisurely stroll to get there. With just nine miles to tick off before the day ended, and nine pretty easy miles at that, we could afford to take it easy and relax.

So whilst some walkers might be rushing and

hurrying on the stretch to Alston, we could linger and take in the sights that the section had to offer.

"Oooh! A scrapyard," Catherine exclaimed as we passed a plot full of rusting machinery tucked behind a fence on the edges of Garrigill village.

Perhaps there was something to rushing through to Alston after all.

* * *

The Pennine Way's journey to Alston follows the South Tyne River, one of the two rivers that come together to create the Tyne River. Cunningly – or perhaps, rather unimaginatively – the other river is called the North Tyne.

The South Tyne would be our bedfellow for most of the day up to Slaggyford. Not always directly next to it, but close enough to see it. And as if there wasn't enough water with the river, it began to rain.

I leaned against a tree and struggled into my waterproofs as fast as possible, rejoicing in my decision to buy a new pair, which – unlike my previous set – could be put on without having to take my walking boots off. The previous ones had always been a nightmare, purchased on the basis of an amazingly low price. It was only when I'd tried to get them for the first time in anger that I realised the folly of my cheapness, and the sheer utter stupidity of the design. When you're out in the countryside and the heavens open the last thing you want to do to is undo your boot laces, remove your footwear and struggle into the trousers, then put your boots back on again, often whilst desperately trying not to fall over into the large pile of mud that you suddenly realise is right behind you. Clearly the person who had designed my old pair had never been out in the countryside when it was raining, yet alone tried to put on their creation whilst rain battered their head.

Mind you, even when my old pair were on, it barely made a difference. Using the cheapest, naffest fabrics, breathability had barely been on the manufacturer's agenda. Walking in them was like walking in your own personal sauna. It didn't take long before the resulting sweat would got me wetter than I would have been if I'd just let the rain soak directly into my normal clothes.

Grateful as I was for my new waterproofs – which generally did their best to keep water out – there was still one thing that expense hadn't solved. The rain still hits your face, generally meaning that you spend all your time looking at the floor, rather than at the views in front of you. As such, the rest of the walk to Alston passed by in a blur of muddy fields and numerous stiles. This was farmland, and the local farmers clearly delighted in making their fields as small as possible, requiring regular crossing between them.

I tried to imagine doing this on a long day walk from Dufton. Of reaching the end of the moorland on the edges of Garrigill, and then suddenly realising that you had another four miles to walk, with field boundaries to traverse every five minutes. I couldn't think of anything that would make me more weary; more desperate to collapse on a bed at 6pm and not get out of it until breakfast time the following morning. And I thought we were having it bad.

* * *

The Pennine Way doesn't feel any need to linger at Alston. It bypasses the town, preferring simply to pop in at its southern tip, and then dart off across the road bridge over the South Tyne. But it was nearly lunch time and it seemed rude not to pay a visit, so we wandered up the road to the town's main street.

Entering the town gave the impression of a place that was perhaps stuck a little in the past. A filling station sign advertised that you could purchase "ICI Petrol" with your "Access Card", which was impressive given ICI had sold its petrol business in 1987, and Access cards became defunct in 1996.

The rest of the town seemed to be on better form. Most of it was built in the 19th century when the town was booming due to the lead mining industry, although when that declined the town survived by focussing on the farming industry. Interestingly, despite being a town at the heart of the North Pennines – and the highest market town in England at that – it barely seemed touched by tourism.

We pottered around the town's main shopping street, and popped in to the outdoor shop to find some gaiters. Whilst our new waterproofs had kept us reasonably dry in the legs and body, our boots were still getting muddy and wet, especially when we were walking on the moorland. We optimistically thought gaiters may assist. And after purchasing some, we headed back outside to find somewhere for lunch.

Alston provided one of those rare things on the Pennine Way: choice. Wandering through the streets we counted at least five lunch options, one of which doubled as a curry house. After much consideration, we picked the Angel based purely on the basis that it had been there since 1611 and had a reasonable sounding menu.

The pub had presumably had some work since it first opened – it didn't exactly look like it had been built in the 17th century – but it was cosy, warm and comfortable. We settled down at a table with two pints, and ordered some food.

It was whilst we were sitting down that we began to notice something rather curious about the Angel's other customers. A window seat was taken up by two seventy year old women supping – of all things – bottles of Smirnoff Ice, whilst at the bar sat a rather spaced out woman who spent most of her time staring into space although at one point she got off her stool, and half-staggered, half-crawled towards the pub's toilets.

We were beginning to feel like we were extras in some sort of bad sitcom; even more so when a group of three lads came in, looked around, engaged in a few minutes of banter with a couple of other people sat at the bar, then headed straight out again without even ordering a single drink. Ten minutes later they were back, and repeated the whole exercise for a second time.

Banter was clearly in order. As we finished our food, the group at the bar spent several minutes trying to wind up the landlord who was sat doing paperwork at a table near us, whilst the rest of the staff rushed around. That he barely raised an eyebrow at the noise heading his way suggested this kind of thing happened here regularly. Watching it all, I resolved that in the highly unlikely event that I was going to write a sitcom set in a pub, I'd head to the Angel for further research.

Much as an afternoon in the Angel was proving increasingly tempting, we had to get on our way and we had much to look forward to once we got back outside. After all, our guide book told us "if there is to be disappointment on any section of the Pennine Way it is likely to be found on the long walk from Alston through Slaggyford and by Lambly to Greenhead."

High praise indeed.

There's a hint of inevitability that, when you create a walk snaking 256 miles up the country, you'll hit some dull sections. But the guide book seemed to be especially harsh on what was to come. I mean, this was a book that had barely blinked about the boggy, dull morass coming down from Tan Hill. Could the few miles that lay ahead of us be really that bad? There was only one way to find out.

It turned out that it perhaps wasn't the finest

part of the Pennine Way, although it also didn't feature a scrapyard. The route took us through a succession of waterlogged fields, each entered by a stile surrounded by copious amounts of mud. Each field seemed to be little different to its predecessor; some soggy grass and the odd sheep who seemed indifferent to our presence. At least they were until one particular field where all the sheep seemed to magically gravitate towards Catherine, who ended leading them Pied-Piper style as far as she could. Desperate attempts to shoo them away failed, and it was only when we reached a footbridge over a stream, that they abandoned their pursuit.

A brass plaque attached to a gate welcomed us to Northumbria, and cryptically added "Isacc's Tea Trail" underneath. Yes, that's right. "Isacc's". Not "Isaac's" but "Isacc's". The typo must have been a slightly expensive mistake to make.

It turned out that Isaac's Tea Trail had been following the Pennine Way since Alston. The 36 mile circular walk has apparently been described by someone as "England's last great undiscovered wilderness trek", although who knows who that someone was, because it was one of those quotes that never seems to be attributed. Perhaps it was Geoff at the local council who said it. Or maybe Martha who works in a lumber merchants. That was probably likely given the lack of a source. If it had been Julia Bradbury or Wainwright, you can bet their name would be plastered all over the posters. But if your killer quote came from Lyndsey in accounts, that might be something you feel the need to hide. And with a billing like that though, it was clear that Isaac's Tea Trail was the walk to do if you thought that the Pennine Way was too urban.

The Tea Trail is a walk named after former lead miner Isaac Holden was hit by a double whammy of falling ill and then losing his job when the mines closed, and falling ill. So Isaac found himself a new career as a door-step purveyor of tea. After converting to Methodism, he began combining his tea business with raising money for the area's poor, and building wells, libraries and a "penny savings bank"; the latter being one of a number of institutions at the time where the poor where encouraged to save money in order to avoid a life in the workhouse.

The man clearly deserved a walking trail after him. Less pleasant in our minds was the farmer just over the county boundary whose field was a veritable sea of mud. It looked like someone had spent a happy afternoon driving their tractor around in circles whilst manically cackling "I'll show those walkers, mwhahahahahahaha!" It was more than possible that the hugely churned up field wasn't a deliberate act, but it certainly didn't give the impression that the landowner was particularly friendly to people crossing their land.

If there was a desire to put people off using the footpath, it wasn't going to be helped by the presence of Whitley Castle nearby. Built by the Romans, probably to protect Alston and its nearby lead mines, only the ramparts now remain, resulting in there being just a series of grassy mounds to explore, although exploration would be punctured by the dry stone walls which criss-crossed the old fort; a sign that for centuries, history was just that. Something that was in the past, and not particularly worth worrying about in the here and now. Although to be fair, the place does just look like a big lump in the ground, so perhaps that's not totally surprising.

Another rallying cry could be found on the path just a short way away. "Kirkstyle Inn (Knarsdale)" said the sign. "Last pub till Greenhead."

No pub on the Pennine Way for 11 miles after the Kirkstyle? This was important news. Especially as we would be in need of refreshment after this long and exhausting day. We just had to get there, and preferably stay mud free, which was proving to be easier said than done. Our brand new gaiters were already proving their worth, and were absolutely coated in brown muck thanks to the churned up fields, as well as stiles and gates which were inevitably surrounded by large pools of muddy water. It was almost impossible to stay even reasonably dry, yet alone clean.

As if to taunt us, right below us there was clearly an easier way. For it's not just the Pennine Way which passes through the area. Running roughly parallel is the South Tyne Trail, which ran flat, straight and looked pretty mud free.

We'd been able to see the South Tyne Trail in the distance for most of the afternoon, but now as we arrived at Kirkhaugh we were suddenly within metres of it. And would remain so for several miles. Its simplicity came from it following an old railway line that had closed in 1976 after the decision to close it was, yet again, suggested in the Beeching report.

Whilst the South Tyne Trail follows an old railway track, it also runs alongside a railway too. Attempts were made to buy the old railway trackbed at the time of closure, but they were to no avail, and barely had the railway been closed than workers were out lifting the track. Undeterred, the preservation movement did succeed in returning railways to the area, creating a narrow gauge railway running from its base in Alston. For a few miles the railway and the path run alongside each other, with a fence in-between for safety reasons.

No doubt had the Pennine Way not pre-dated the railway's closure, it would have been diverted along the old railway line instead of the rather random and ramshackle route over farmland it actually follows. All of which means that the Pennine Way walker can only look on at the simplicity and dryness of their neighbour, and wish they'd had the foresight to follow the old railway instead.

A prime example of the difference between the two came just before the hamlet of Slaggyford. After spending much of the day looking down on the South Tyne Trail from the sides of a hill, suddenly we were heading below it; our path taking a turn to pass under an old railway viaduct. For good measure, our route consisted mostly of slippery mud, heading steeply downhill. It was clearly not the best of routes; something confirmed by the presence of a single gaiter strapped to a gate, which had clearly been lost in a desperate tussle between hiker and path. And if there wasn't enough mud to look at, the area also seemed to be strewn with rabbit corpses just for good measure.

Despite only having had a relatively short distance to walk for the day, the conditions underfoot were such that it had been a pretty tiring day and our arrival in Slaggyford was more than welcome. We were staying in an old chapel, beautifully converted into a fantastically decorated building, complete with former chapel features. Even the chapel's old pulpit had found its place in the refurbishment. Despite being incredibly wet and covered nearly head to toe in the old brown stuff, we were warmly greeted and swiftly plied with tea and biscuits. The response of Pennine Way B&B owners to the bedraggled, muddy people who arrived on their doorsteps never failed to amaze me, especially those that were – like our abode for this night – immaculately decorated. I always faintly expected that someone would open the door, take one look at us, shriek "Eeurrrgh!" before promptly slamming the door in our faces. It never happened. Although it would be hard to imagine any accommodation provider on the Pennine Way staying in business for long if they objected to a little mud here and there.

There was however a slight downside to our glorious home from home: the lack of a pub. This was to our surprise as we'd understood there was one nearby. Our pre-walk research – which had mostly consisted of typing "Slaggyford pub" into a well known internet search engine – had returned the Kirkstyle Inn on the results page. The online map on said search engine had even showed it to be within a short distance of our B&B.

There was just one problem. The internet was wrong. The Kirkstyle Inn may have had Slaggyford in its address, but it was actually over a mile up a busy road from the village itself, with no pavement to walk on.

Still, the last pub before Greenhead was one that would need to be savoured and enjoyed. And it could perhaps only be enjoyed after a little effort had been exerted in order to get there. Although as it happened we put no effort in. By sheer coincidence, a friend of the B&B's owners had been visiting them, and was going to be driving past the pub at exactly the same time we wanted to go. Talk about good timing.

Despite being in the middle of nowhere, the Kirkstyle was heaving. Pints were being supped, and food was coming out of the pub's kitchen quick and fast, and we only just managed to blag ourselves a table as we settled down for the evening. Clearly that faded advertisement on the route of the Pennine Way was paying off for the owners. And we certainly weren't going to argue. We may have been on our second pub of the day, but we still had the previous pub-less evening to make up for.

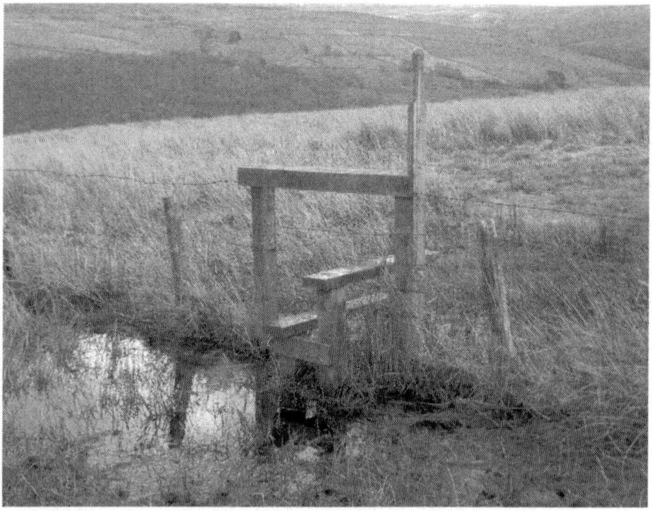

Slaggyford to Greenhead

It was a rare night on any of our Pennine Way travels that we didn't stay somewhere reasonably close to the trail. Yes, there were a couple of nights which had a bit of a trek. And there was one night that involved a car and a motorway. But generally we stayed within a mile or so of the path itself.

And that's fine. But sometimes there was something even better. Those were the days when we could simply step out of the door of our B&B or hostel, and find ourselves instantly on the Pennine Way.

Our B&B at Slaggyford provided us with one such morning. The B&B even had a Pennine Way signpost right next to the front door. A front door that, incidentally, had doves nesting near it. One particular dove had taken it upon herself to build her nest on top of a small ornament mounted on the wall, right above the front door. Not the most obvious place to bring up your young chick, although she seemed happy with the arrangement, and barely batted an eyelid (or whatever the dove equivalent is) as we opened the door and stepped out onto the pavement right in front of her.

Two Pennine Way walkers first thing in the morning? She'd obviously seen it all before.

* * *

The Pennine Way once again ran almost parallel to the South Tyne Trail, and would be doing for a couple of miles. And yet again, the other trail looked far nicer than our own. Within minutes of leaving Slaggyford we were heading along yet another veritable mudfest, whilst mere metres away lay a pristine path, in perfect condition.

"Maybe we should think about taking a detour over there," I suggested to Catherine as we squelched and slid around on the Pennine Way.

It seemed like a good plan, although the silence I received in reply suggested the sanctity of the Pennine Way route was frankly far more important than the fact that we might be getting a little dirty.

At least at Burnstones our torment would be over, for it is here that the two trails begin to diverge. The South Tyne Trail goes off towards the town of Haltwhistle, whilst the Pennine Way heads in a slightly different direction towards the village of Greenhead. That didn't mean we'd left the railway behind completely. We would be walking within half a mile of the old railway line for a few more miles yet, but at least it wouldn't be right next to us, taunting us with its path of finest stones; smooth, easy going and problem free.

We were well on our way to what is perhaps the historical highlight of the Pennine Way. For at Greenhead, the trail arrives at the remains of Hadrian's Wall and many other Roman fortifications that have long since passed into decay. To get there we had to follow part of an old Roman road named Maiden Way. That, incidentally, is probably not the name the Romans gave to the road. The actual Roman names for all their roads in Britain have been long lost. The names we use now to describe them are derived from the Anglo-Saxon language, given to the roads after the Romans had left Britain for good. Even then, we don't quite know why the Anglo-Saxons chose that name, although its likely that it was named for "Maiden Castle"; this being a name given to many castles and forts and believed to mean "impregnable looking castle." So, nothing about unmarried women at all.

These days you won't find soldiers marching down the road. They stopped bothering with it many years ago. However, the path has found itself a new role marking the boundary between moorland and lush green farmland; the two divided by a dry stone wall.

The Maiden Way ran along on the moorland side of the boundary, and any hope that following an old Roman road would provide us with good walking conditions were swiftly discarded as we began to squelch our way over bogs, and jump majestically over giant puddles. Stiles were especially affected. One was surrounded by so much water that it was physically impossible to even get close to it without finding ourselves up to our knees in water. In the end we had to resort to climbing over a barbed wire fence in order to cross over into the next field and stay dry.

The previous night we'd been told by a local that there'd barely been any rain recently; at least until

– just our luck – a few days before our arrival when the heavens had opened in style. The moors certainly were showing the affects of the downpours. A substantial amount of the path had been turned into mini-ponds, some of them even had some wildlife in them.

"What's that in there?" I said, stopping abruptly and staring intently into the murky water.

Catherine stopped and wandered over to peer over my shoulder.

"That's frog spawn, isn't it?" I added.

"Yep, I think so."

"So the local frogs have been up here and decided that this small puddle is the perfect place for their young to grow."

"That certainly does seem to be the case," and we stared at each other and marvelled at the wonders of nature.

* * *

Our guidebook was as equally dismissive of this section as it had been of our walk between Alston and Slaggyford, which seemed a little harsh. True, this wasn't the stand-out scenery of the Yorkshire Dales or Kinder Scout, but there was nothing intrinsically bad about it. It even featured a ruined barn at High House. How can a stretch of a walk which includes a ruined barn possibly be bad? I just can't imagine. It's really just not possible. The barn seemed like a perfect place to stop for some lunch. And it was for about five seconds, until a strong and extremely cold wind began to blow in our direction, instantly persuading us to move on.

Despite it being a Sunday, we had the area to ourselves. Not once did we exchange pleasantries with a single other person, in that way that walkers do, and the only other walkers we saw all day were two people in the distance who were walking on the South Tyne Trail. Instead, our company came mostly in the form of sheep, some with recently born lambs who lay close to their mothers in the grassy fields.

After a dalliance with farmland, we arrived on Hartleyburn Common; a large expanse of hair moss and thick green grass. We were on the common, and its neighbour, Blenkinsopp Common, for over an hour, but it felt far longer. The flat landscape offered few views, just repetitive visions of moorland stretching out in front of us.

Finally, on the edge of the common came Black Hill with its views of farmland below. We were edging towards Greenhead, and Hadrian's Wall country, but first there was a golf course to walk through. Yes, here in the heart of Hadrian's Wall country, in a rural location where the nearest and largest town around has a population of a mere 3,000 people, can be found the 18 hole Haltwhistle Golf Course. It's quite possibly the only golf course to be sited on an old Roman camp, with ramparts, ditches and the works. You really don't get that kind of thing in a golf course in Surrey now, do you?

Most of our Roman exploration would take place

on the next two days, but our journey into Greenhead would take us past one piece of Roman remains: the Vallum. A long ditch, built sometime after Hadrian's Wall, the Vallum's purpose has never been fully explained, although it is believed by many to be a boundary marker; that the long ditch formed the southern boundary of a military zone, which ran northwards to the wall. Perhaps just installing a fence wasn't deemed to be obvious enough to people. Although it would, I am sure, have been far easier to erect. We walked along the ditch, sorry, the Vallum, a short way before leaving the Pennine Way for Greenhead and our accommodation. There would be plenty of time for Romans in the morning after all.

We were staying in another converted chapel, this time in a hostel that was based in the buildings. The former Methodist chapel had opened to worshippers in 1885, before finally closing its doors in 1974. In prime walkers country, the building hadn't remained empty for long, and was swiftly converted into accommodation by the YHA who opened it up for business in 1978.

The YHA had however caused us some mild panic. We'd booked our beds two months earlier, making the booking by phone due to the YHA's online booking system not working properly for some reason. Whilst on the phone we learned that the hostel had had some flooding problems, but they assured us that they were working on it and fully expected to be re-opening by the time we'd arrived. However they promised to let us know if there was a problem.

There we left it, until days before we left London when I was scouring the YHA website trying to find out the hostel's address and contact details, so that we'd have them with us in case of any problems; something I did for everywhere we planned to stay. I fired up the website and found the Greenhead page.

"This location has now closed." said the YHA website rather bluntly.

Woah, wait a minute, what? Closed? What? Why? How? Why had no one told us? Where on earth were we going to stay?! Could the flooding really have been that bad that they'd simply walked away from the place?

I began to run around the room in circles; flapping my arms around for good measure. This was a problem. This wasn't good. Would we be able to find somewhere to stay in time? It was March, a time when many B&B owners head off on their own holidays due to it being rather quiet out there.

Within minutes I was frantically searching the YHA's website, wondering how a hostel could be closed so quickly. And found nothing. Not one thing. At least I couldn't, until I logged in to the website's forums. And there it was. Buried in a page that was completely invisible unless you'd bothered to sign up to the forums and had then logged in.

"For members and guests information. From January 1st YHA Greenhead will cease to be involved in the YHA's Enterprise scheme."

I clearly wasn't the only one going "Huh?" with a confused look on my face at this completely cryptic, incomprehensible message. Another user had left the reply:

"Err.... sorry, but what on earth does 'cease to be involved in the YHA's Enterprise scheme' mean? Something to do with Star Trek? Why is it 'leaving the network'?"

It turned out that the YHA, in their wisdom, had decided to flog the hostel a few years earlier. It had been put on the market, and sold to the owners of the nearby Greenhead Hotel who had kept it open as a hostel and had initially decided to operate it under the YHA's franchise scheme, which is strangely called "Enterprise" for reasons that I'm sure seem obvious to someone, but not me.

For whatever reason, Greenhead had then later decided to leave the YHA network; the decision being implemented a few months before our visit. The place was still open as an independent hostel, however the YHA had decided to paste up a completely incorrect and misleading message on their website.

All they had to do was put a message up saying "Greenhead Hostel is no longer part of the YHA" and all this would have been at least a little clearer. And for that matter, would have saved me from wearing a circular hole in the carpet due to worry and panic. At least it was all, finally, explained but it did cause some unnecessary angst.

Back at Greenhead, we checked in to the hostel

and found our room. The place smelt faintly of fresh paint, and was completely deserted. There was not even a member of staff on site; we'd had to get our key from the hotel over the road.

It was the first night open after being closed for the winter season; the first night as an independent hostel, and we were the only two people wandering around a place that could accommodate 40. It was an eerie feeling, wandering around empty corridors, passing rooms that would no doubt be full later in the year, but for now seemed like they were sleeping.

We contemplated doing all those things that you can do when in a large building by yourself; running around the corridors screaming, jumping on all the beds, re-arranging all the pans in the communal kitchen. That sort of thing. But instead we had a cup of tea before heading across the road and had a pint in the hotel. Those pans really could wait until the morning.

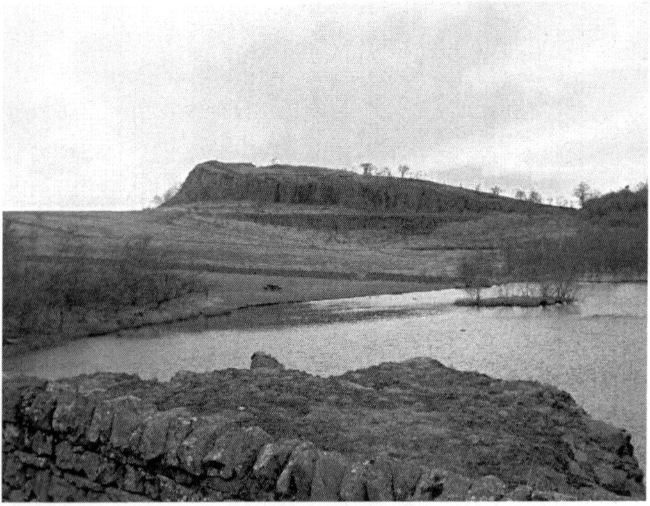

Greenhead to Once Brewed

"Only six and a half miles to do tomorrow. Shall we have a lie in?" Catherine suggested, as we supped bottles of local ale in the Greenhead Hotel.

I thought for a moment, before deciding, why on earth not? There was no real need to get up early. We had a few bits and bats we could eat for breakfast so we didn't need to rush over to the hotel at 8am to get some food, and the short distance to Once Brewed hostel could be easily achieved in a few hours. This would leave us with plenty of time to poke around Roman remains, stop off at a pub for lunch and still arrive at our evening's accommodation before the sun set. It may be a walking trip, but we were on holiday after all. So why not spend a little time resting and relaxing?

And so we did. Rather than our normal routine of hitting the road by nine – half past if the B&B only did later breakfasts – it was well after ten by the time we returned to the Pennine Way, which seemed frankly wrong. But then, that's the whole point of a lie in.

Back outside and it was time to discover the history of the area. And what better place to start a tour of the remains of Roman Britain than Thirwell Castle, which is a 12th century castle that was – cunningly – home to the Thirwell family. And I know what you're thinking. That's not very Roman is it? Well that's where you'd be wrong, for after it was built the castle was strengthened using stones nabbed from nearby Hadrian's Wall. Well, it's a connection.

The castle began to fall into disrepair in the 18th century, and suffered several major collapses of masonry, including one in 1982. These days it's maintained by the Northumberland National Park Authority, has been made safe, and is open to the public to wander around, which is exactly what we did. The extent of the decay is such that it's hard to imagine what the place was like originally. Here was a building where people lived. Children were no doubt born, and ran around this place, but now it was just a pile of stones.

Back outside the castle walls, we returned to the Vallum, following it to Walltown Quarry, which is now a country park complete with the obligatory picnic area, car park and lake. Again, this may not sound very Roman, but stick with it. Opened in 1877, the quarry was opened to extract whinstone, a hard, very durable rock used for building roads. As the road network expanded, demand for whinstone grew and Walltown's output was even used to build the M6 motorway around Penrith.

The Romans never quarried whinstone – it was far too hard to extract in that era and it was only until after the industrial revolution that the technology became available to extract it. However, just because they couldn't quarry it didn't mean that the Romans didn't make use of it. The whinstone ridge was used to help make Hadrian's

Wall an even stronger barrier. But centuries later that also caused a problem. Hadrian's Wall got in the way of quarrying.

Although it had been raided for building materials for centuries after the Romans left Britain, by the Victorian era there was increasing concern over damage to Hadrian's Wall, so much so that in 1834 there was a move to buy up sections of land in order to protect it. Awareness of the issue had been growing steadily when the quarry opened some forty years later. An attempt to extend Walltown Quarry in the 1950s was successfully defeated, but it wasn't until 1977 that Walltown finally closed its doors, and after many more years, opened up into the country park it is now.

There were already a few people pottering around Walltown as we arrived at the car park. A bus stop opposite the public toilets informed us that the local bus service was numbered "AD122 bus" – a nod to the year that construction of Hadrian's Wall is believed to have commenced. Near it, an information panel with a map of the whole of Hadrian's Wall, seemed slightly confused as it offered not one, but two arrows claiming "You are here." Apparently we could either have been at Walltown, or at Bowness-on-Solway on the Cumbrian coast. We looked around, just to check we couldn't see the sea and therefore hadn't got hopelessly lost since we'd left Greenhead, and were extremely reassured to discover that our navigational skills weren't quite that bad.

From the car park it was clear to see where a

huge chunk of the whinstone had been removed, just a metre or so short of a section of wall, which ran behind the quarrying line. This was to be our first encounter with Hadrian's Wall; a landmark we'd spend most of the day with. Naturally we headed over to take a look.

Like many people seeing Hadrian's Wall for the first time, I felt slightly lacking in awe at it. In my mind, it was a tall, straight monster of a thing, not a little runt barely a few rows of bricks high. For some reason too, I'd envisioned the whole thing as being on a long, flat stretch of ground, whereas it was clear that it in real life, the wall had been built on undulating ground.

The Pennine Way – now heading along with a fellow National Trail, the Hadrian's Wall Path – stuck close to the wall, bouncing up and down as it moved along. Here and there the wall showed a little more of its former glory, with a height higher than myself, although still some way from the 3m in height that it apparently once rose above the ground. Other times though, such as at another former quarry, it disappeared completely with next to nothing of it remaining. The lower – and sometimes non-existent – wall height did at least have one benefit, allowing the walker to get great views north, as well as south.

Such was the demand of whinstone, that there were several quarries in the area and we came across another closed site, two miles on from Walltown. Cawfields Quarry has again been opened up to the public, the only sign of its old life was a small hill that had essentially been half removed. It was a curious sight; like someone had just come down with a large knife and cut off half of it and taken it away. Which, in essence, I guess they had.

Cawfields was also where we could grab some lunch so we headed off the short distance to the nearby Milecastle public house. It was ideal timing mainly because after having only had a light breakfast we were both ravenous, but also because it had just started raining. We had no idea when they would stop serving lunch, but it was half one so it seemed to be a good bet that we'd be able to get a bite to eat. Sure enough, a large sign outside informed us that the place served food until 3. With a skip and a jump, we went in.

The Milecastle was heaving, full of people making their way through large plates that were positively groaning with food. We looked at each other excitedly, ordered a pint at the bar and found a table from where we could study the large menu displayed on a blackboard on the wall. After swiftly agreeing, Catherine went up to order.

"The kitchen closed at half two," came the blunt reply from the other side of the bar, in sharp contrast to the large sign outside.

Well, yes. But as it was 1:40 that was fine, surely? There was a blank and distinctly unhelpful stare from the other side of the bar. And then we saw a clock.

2:40.

Back at the table, we looked at our watches

completely baffled. And then it hit me.

"The clocks went forward last night, didn't they?"

We hadn't left the hostel at quarter past ten. Our lie-in had lasted an hour longer. And now, hungry and damp, our inability to remember that the weekend marked the change to British Summer Time meant our lunch would have to consist of a pint of ale and a packet of crisps; this after being told by the distinctly unhelpful bar staff that the only other food locally would be at the Twice Brewed Inn three miles up the road, right next to the hostel we were aiming for.

Still, whilst hungry, at least we could relax and dry out in the warmth.

"Last orders please!" came a bored shout from behind the bar, and within minutes the staff at the Milecastle were doing their best to hustle us out of the building in a way that suggested they clearly couldn't wait to get rid of everyone. We downed our drinks as fast as we could and went to the door. Barely had we set foot outside and it was slammed shut behind us; the sound of bolts being rapidly drawn, more than audible.

"Pub closing at 3pm on a Sunday. What decade are we in again?" I said as we headed back towards the road.

Catherine abruptly stopped.

"My gloves!" she cried.

On entering the pub we'd taken off our muddy walking boots and left them in the pub's small porch. This would mean we wouldn't trample dirt onto their carpet. Although, given the service there, part of me wished we hadn't bothered. This naturally meant that we'd had to put our boots back on as we left the building. In doing so, Catherine had placed her rucksack on the floor, and had put her gloves on the porch's window ledge for a moment whilst tying her laces. In the rush that the staff had created in order to boot us out into the cold, she'd neglected to pick them up again. Now they sat on the window ledge, plain for all to see, but completely inaccessible to us.

Given we'd had several cold days already, and were expecting some more, there was no way Catherine was going to leave her gloves on a pub's window ledge, and we set about trying to retrieve them. Short of throwing a brick through a window – which we suspected wouldn't go down particularly well – there were few options available to us. We needed to try and raise someone from inside the pub.

We wandered round the building, trying to find a doorbell, a knocker, anything that would raise the alarm. Surely the pub must have delivery people trying to get in sometimes? But there was nothing. Likewise there was no sign of a phone number we could ring. All of which meant we had little choice but to stand outside in the rain shouting at the windows in the hope that someone would notice.

It took ten minutes but eventually someone showed up, glared at us and begrudging opened the door, allowing us just enough time to retrieve the offending gloves before it was swiftly slammed again in our faces.

"Such lovely people," I muttered as we left, hoping there was nothing else left inside that we'd need to retrieve.

* * *

We continued along the undulating path alongside the wall, past the remains of a milecastle, one of the small forts that were built every mile along the wall. A Roman mile that is: a measurement slightly shorter than the modern imperial length.

Eighty milecastles were built, each manned by between 20 and 30 guards. As well as being a defensive position, each also acted as a crossing point across the frontier, and as a customs post. Each milecastle then had two turrets, positioned a third of a mile away on each side. Coupled with the turrets maintained by the next milecastle, the result was that there'd be lookout and monitoring facilities every third of a mile; more than enough to give a good view over a wide area.

That afternoon the Pennine Way would take us past Milecastles 42 and 41, according to a numbering system introduced in 1930, which runs with 1 in the east and 80 in the west. Little remained of Milecastle 42, besides some low walls, although this is far more than Milecastle 41, and – indeed – most other milecastles, which now are long gone. Looking at it, it was incredible to think how much effort had gone into building Hadrian's Wall and its associated structures. Building the wall alone took six years, and whilst several attempts were made to push the Roman border further into what is now Scotland, it remained the northernmost part of the Roman Empire until the Romans left Britain in 410 AD.

It was hard not to wonder what it must have been like to be stationed up here, next to this cold, slightly bleak-looking moorland day in, day out. And as I did so, it began to rain again.

Thankfully we were only a short way from Once Brewed, which meant we were also only a short distance from actually obtaining something to eat and maybe even a warm drink. But in getting there, we'd get utterly drenched. The rain was coming down big style – almost hailstones – and the water bounced dramatically as it hit the tarmac.

Soaked to the bone, we staggered into Once Brewed YHA, desperately wanting to check in quickly, find our room and change swiftly into some dry clothes.

It wasn't to be. For starters we were firmly stuck in a queue behind a family who seemed to be the slowest people in the world. Slow to answer every question posed to them; slow to fill in the registration forms; slow to move their backsides and get out of their way. We couldn't even get some space to take off our waterproofs thanks to their several children taking up all the benches that lined the reception area. By the time they'd finally left we'd been stood wearily for ten minutes, and a huge puddle had formed on the floor underneath our feet.

We dragged ourselves down the hostel's corridors and found our twin room, where we found a pair of beds that gave every impression that they'd been created by someone sawing a bunkbed in half. Horizontally of course. Quickly drying ourselves off, and loading up the hostel's drying room with our clothes, we raced down the road to the Twice Brewed Inn.

There are several stories behind the pub's name, some referring to the strength of beer; that "once brewed" ale was too weak, whilst the beer brewed at the pub was "twice brewed" and thus stronger. A less alcoholic reason, given in a newspaper article, is that the name comes from "the unmistakable sight of Hadrian's Wall snaking across the brows – or "brews" – of two hills where there is also a meeting of a pair of drovers' roads."

Naturally the inquisitive may wonder why, therefore, the hostel is known as "Once Brewed". A plaque in the hostel's reception answered that question for us. Someone cleverly decided that if there was a Twice Brewed, then there really needed to be a "Once Brewed" as well.

Well it made sense to someone I guess.

Still, the Twice Brewed – or Twicey as it seemed to be affectionately known – offered everything you'd want in a pub, which also meant that it offered everything we'd failed to get earlier in the day. A roaring fire, a menu positively groaning with great sounding options, and a bar loaded with local ales. Oh and the service was good too.

What else could we possibly need? And having

barely eaten all day, it was certainly time to tuck in. Which we did with gusto.

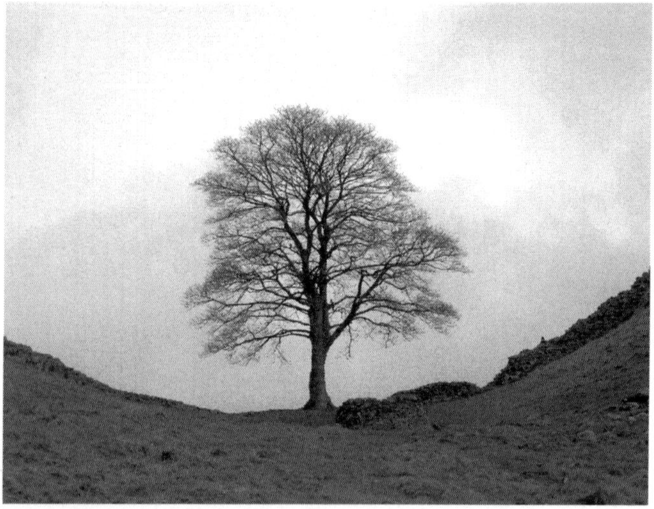

Once Brewed to Bellingham

We woke to the sound of rain hitting the hostel window. And hitting it hard.

Now this need not be always a sign that the day is going to be gloomy and miserable. The year before, I had gone on a walking trip in Cumbria. Every morning, at around 5am, I'd been woken by the sound of the poor weather outside, yet by the time I'd risen from my bed at around eight, the sun had come out and the Lake District was looking absolutely gorgeous, with barely a cloud in the sky. But let's be honest here. That's not something that happens often. And it certainly wasn't going to happen to us at Once Brewed.

It was with reluctance that we left the warmth (and dryness) of the YHA and returned to the Pennine Way. But what better a way to start a day of walking than immediately leaping onto the path right next to Hadrian's Wall.

We had another couple of miles walking in the company of Hadrian's endeavour, with the trail taking us past the remains of more milecastles and turrets. At one point the wall went up a particularly undulating section, requiring the path to make some steep climbs up and then back down into a small dip, before rising up once more.

Then, at one dip, the wall disappeared, replaced instead by a tree. Based on the number of photographs of this particular tree I'd seen in the Twice Brewed Inn and at Greenhead, the tree at Sycamore Gap must be one of the most photographed parts of the wall. Perhaps this was less related to the fact that it was in a rather picturesque spot, and more to do with the fact that the tree had been featured in the film Robin Hood: Prince of Thieves. There was no denying we were in an attractive place though, and my camera lens clicked and whirred as I attempted to take my own shot of this local landmark. And all without Kevin Costner anywhere to be seen.

* * *

Sometimes the wall was in good condition, other times less so. There were, however, occasions when the lack of a wall wasn't too much of a worry. There were other things to see. As we passed through the curiously named Hotbank Farm, a cow seemed to be looking distinctly uncomfortable as it lay down on the side of the ditch, some way from the rest of the herd.

For a moment we wondered whether we should head to the farmhouse to tell someone that there was a cow in distress, when suddenly it all became clear. The cow was about to give birth.

Retreating to a respectful distance away – naturally being careful not to appear threatening to the mother – we watched as a new calf was brought into the world. For a moment it lay still, before beginning to slowly roll down the side of the ditch;

its mother nuzzling it and licking its face. It was soon jerking around and trying to get on its feet, and then it was up and away; its mum happy that all was looking good.

The big moment completed, we pushed on to Rapishaw Gap where a ladder stile would take us over the wall, and a path would take us off onto the distinctly flat plains of the Barbarian lands to the north. But not the lands of Scotland. Whilst some sections of Hadrian's Wall get reasonably close to the modern border, a lot of the time Scotland is far further away. From where we stood, we were forty or so miles away from the nearest Scottish town, and any Barbarians seeking to invade right now would more likely be coming from Northumbria rather than Scotland.

A mile of walking through rain sodden moorland was then followed by a complete change of character for the Pennine Way as it passed into Wark Forest. After the muddy, boggy paths of much of the last few days, the chance to walk on even wetter and boggier forest tracks, was more than welcome.

With just 62 people per square kilometre, Northumberland is one of the least populated parts of England. This meant that when the UK government decided to expand the country's forests following depletion during World War I, the county of Northumberland was an obvious place to start tree planting. Wark Forest is the southern part of the much larger Kielder Forest; a massive entity that is the largest managed by the Forestry

Commission, and that supplies a whopping 25% of all the wood produced in the whole of the UK. And all on an area of land that comes in at 65,000 hectares. To put that into the units that seem to be near compulsory to use when talking about area, that's more than 91,000 football pitches. Kielder Forest in itself covers 13% of the entire county of Northumberland. And that's ignoring all the other forests in the county.

Yes, it's a big forest all right. And one we'd spend a fair amount of time in later in our journey. Our introduction to it lasted a mere mile and a half before we were ejected out onto a patch of moorland known as Haughton Common. Bordered by the spruce trees on three sides, it seemed a quiet and distinctly empty place, hardly encouraging anyone to linger, and we pushed on as quickly as we could. Yet despite the emptiness, there was life here.

On the other side of the Common, we could see another walker heading towards us.

Any Pennine Way walker who has set off from the bright lights of Edale will be used to seeing other walkers. They're everywhere. Even on the most miserable day, you'll still find some mad fool decked out in waterproofs doing a day hike round the hill tops. You'll always see someone out there, no matter what day it is, or whether its bright sunshine or pouring down with rain.

Yet the further north you head on the trail, the fewer people you begin to see. Because it's a slow reduction, occurring over many, many miles, the change is almost imperceptible. At least it is until you spend a whole day out walking and realise you haven't seen anyone since you paid your B&B bill at 9am that morning, and now it's half four in the afternoon.

It's a change that is completely inevitable. The Pennine Way starts within spitting distance of several major urban conurbations, but slowly and surely it gets more and more remote. There's a blip when you approach Hadrian's Wall due to it being a major tourist attraction, and then you leave it behind and are alone again.

We'd obviously set off too early for most of the visitors to the Wall that day as we hadn't seen anyone at all since we'd left Once Brewed, and obviously once we left it, we hadn't seen a soul. Until now that was. And they were walking, slowly but surely towards us.

There was a fence and a stile in the middle of the moor, and we were all heading towards it. As we walked towards it, we wondered who would get there first? Us or them? The tension was mounting as we got closer and closer; all would soon be revealed in spectacular fashion when all three of us pretty much arrived at the stile at exactly the same time.

Now I can't speak for our fellow walker, but we certainly hadn't varied our pace in any way, in order to make this amazing coincidence happen. And it was an outstanding coincidence. The only three people out hiking in the area – perhaps for many miles around – all meeting up at the same stile, creating a mini-traffic jam as we each tried to cross from one side to the other.

Like us, he was walking the Pennine Way, although, unlike us he, was walking north to south. Having set off from Kirk Yetholm a few days earlier, his plan was to head as far south as the weather would allow him to get. He was hoping to get to Edale, but cautious given he hadn't particularly had particularly great conditions so far. Well, absolutely. What kind of fool would walk the Pennine Way in March after all?

After learning from him that the paths ahead of us were just a bit boggy, and him learning from us that the paths ahead of him were, well, just a bit boggy, we wished him good luck, bade him farewell and headed on our way.

A little way ahead of us sat a sheepfold, designed in such a way to ensure that any sheep, or passing humans for that matter, could take shelter from any strong winds that happened to be blowing at the time. Our guide book enthused about the structure, letting us know that "this makes an acceptable stopping point for lunch, though the desolation of the place may cause you to hasten on your way." High praise indeed. But still, it was lunchtime and we hadn't seen many better places to stop and rest so we popped inside to find that yes, it was indeed pretty sheltered.

Unfortunately it was also almost completely full of sheep poo. It seemed that every sheep in the area had popped over to for some rest and shelter, and had naturally made use of the area for other purposes too. There was barely any space free to sit down on that wasn't covered in greeny-brown pellets. Not that it really mattered, as no sooner had we reached the sheepfold than it started raining again. And the last thing you really want when eating your sandwich, is for it to get soggy and wet.

"Anyway," I said to Catherine as we set off once more, "It's far too desolate for my liking."

* * *

Another forest section was over almost as soon as it began, and it was followed by a trek down a road that took us past an establishment that proclaimed itself to be "the North East's premier bonsai nursery." That's for growing miniature trees, not miniature humans of course.

With the rain continuing, we huddled under some trees on the edge of another stretch of forest in order to eat our lunch, and made our way on another section of boggy moorland. It was becoming abundantly clear that we'd picked the wrong time of year to be walking the Pennine Way. The weather had been getting worse by the day, the scenery certainly wasn't looking its best and the ground clearly wasn't coping well with the influx of water bashing down on it. But we'd made our bed, and we'd have to lie in it. It was Kirk Yetholm or bust. Or more accurately, Kirk Yetholm or drown trying.

This unfortunately required an afternoon

wandering around in some dreary conditions with waterproof jacket hoods hoisted firmly over our heads, and rain seeping further and further into our boots. There was little we could do other than just plod on and take what moments of respite that could be provided.

One such – rare – moment came in a field at Lowstead Farm. The Pennine Way had taken us through a number of fields, one of which was the home of two very friendly lambs which jumped up at us, and frolicked around our legs as we tried to walk; all under the gaze of their mother who seemed to be watching with a distinct look of maternal pride.

Leaving the sheep to their field, we pushed on down tracks and roads to Shitlington Hall – in reality a rather grandly named farmhouse – and then to nearby Shitlington Crag; names that only the highly immature would find amusing. Honest. The crag is a local landmark; a series of sandstone boulders that stand dramatically, and provide a perfect subject for photography. Not that I was daring to get the camera out to take a photograph. The rain was beginning to ooze through my waterproofs, and despite the fact that I was keeping my camera in a case that itself was in an inside pocket, things were beginning to look distinctly damp and soggy. I was beginning to worry that if things got any worse, I may not only be having to dry out my clothes that night, but also my photography equipment.

By now our boots were so wet that cold water

was freely running around inside them, and every time a foot went down, there was the sound of sploshing and squelching. We stomped miserably through the wet fields, desperately wanting the day to end; to find ourselves in our cosy B&B with a nice cup of tea, and quite possibly a biscuit.

At long last the town of Bellingham came into view. We arrived at a road where a sign informed us that the town offered such essentials as petrol, a giant knife and fork, caravans, tents, beds, toilets and a large, rather curly letter I, and that seemed good enough to us. Even then, it would take us another half hour of walking in order to get to all those exciting features.

We crossed over the swollen River North Tyne – sister river to the South Tyne that now seemed so far away – and made our way towards the town, seeking out our B&B and the location of any convenient pubs.

"Is it this place, which has a jacuzzi," I asked Catherine as we walked past the first B&B we'd come across, and which was happily boasting its many exciting facilities on a large sign.

"No, I don't think so. I think it's this one," she said, pointing to a small cottage whose main sign, in contrast, revealed that the building was for sale.

"Oh my goodness, you're drenched!" came the call from the landlady as the front door was opened. "Come inside into the warm!"

We were ushered inside, and shown to our room so we could change into some dry clothing; all the soggy wet stuff, which was most of what we'd been wearing, was then swiftly dispatched to dry next to the B&B's substantial boiler, which seemed to be more than up for the challenge.

It had been one of those days when you just want to crawl under a duvet and not come out again until breakfast, but somehow we managed to muster enough enthusiasm to head back outside into the rain and find some food. Bellingham seemed to have three pubs and a Chinese takeaway. Yes we were going to be spoiled for choice. Well, at least it seemed like we would.

One of the pubs seemed to be completely deserted; from its run down exterior we weren't even sure it was still in business, yet alone whether it served food or not. A second, with a mock Tudor frontage, looked like a reasonable choice and we stepped inside to find a pub with low beams and a roaring fire. We sidled up to the bar to ask the ultimate question.

"Are you doing food?"

We are indeed," came the call from behind the bar. "Monday night is curry night! It's chicken curry tonight, served with rice and naan."

Ah. We looked at each other, sensing there may be a slight issue.

"Anything vegetarian?" asked Catherine, who had ceased to eat meat some years earlier.

"Err, no," said the barmaid, with a look of surprise on her face that suggested no one had ever asked her this before, and that this not-eating-meat thing was some sort of strange and unusual concept that was completely new to this part of the north east of England.

Well that was that, and we headed out of the door and down the road to the third pub.

The place was mostly deserted, with just a handful of people huddling round a fire that did little more than glow enigmatically in an otherwise cold room. Next to the bar a large TV screen blared out an episode of Emmerdale.

"Are you doing food tonight?" we nervously asked, as we disrupted her viewing.

"Of course," she replied, handing us a ridiculously large menu, and we breathed a huge sigh of relief that we wouldn't have to resort to eating chop suey sat on a bench outside the Co-op that night. "Do you want to eat in here, or in the dining room?"

The main bar was hardly the life and soul of a party, so unless most of the village was in there, it seemed unlikely the dining room would be any major improvement, and the thought of spending our evening in a large room alone by ourselves was even worse.

"In here's fine," we replied, taking a table as close to the fire as we could get without seeming like we were being overly friendly to the two other customers.

Everything about the place suggested the food would probably be disappointing; a view compounded by the fact that it would be the only pub on the whole of the Pennine Way where we were unable to order a pint of real ale. A sign outside had advertised them, however the bar's sole handpull was completely empty, requiring us to resort to pints of over-cold Boddingtons instead.

It wasn't exactly a bad pub – although the Boddies was pretty dire – but the TV screen piping out Emmerdale and Coronation Street just seemed to zap all the life out of the place. The only person watching it was the woman behind the bar who spent most of her time glued to the screen; the few customers who ventured in using up very little of her time. Most weren't even in to drink, and there instead to pick up a take-away pizza that seemed to be the pub's sideline, and which probably yielded higher profits that night than anything else.

It was just all so disappointing. This was to be our last pub until we reached Kirk Yetholm. The next evening would be spent in a tiny, pub free village, and the one after in a remote farmhouse in the middle of nowhere. What we wanted from our penultimate pub of the trip was a cosy village inn, and what we'd got was a standard town pub that could have been anywhere.

True, after we'd eaten our food we couldn't have headed to the curry pub down the road, or maybe even seen if that third pub had bothered to open its doors. But what would the point be? It seemed to be a day that had been set up for disappointment. Terrible weather, miserable pub and no ale. At least tomorrow would be a fresh day. And one that would see us leave Bellingham with no requirement ever to come back.

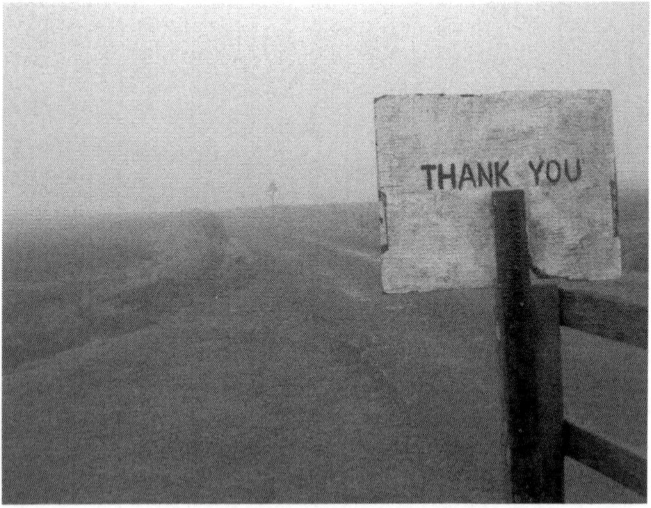
THANK YOU

Bellingham to Byrness

"I'm sorry to ask this, but when you booked I'd forgotten that I have to take my husband for a hospital appointment first thing in the morning. Would you be all right having your breakfast about 7am?"

How do you say no to a request like that? You'd have to be a pretty heartless so and so to refuse. Even if it did mean setting our alarms for an utterly unearthly hour of the morning. I mean, we were supposed to be on holiday...

Radio 2 was blaring out of the radio as we stumbled, bleary eyed, into the dining room in order to eat our freshly cooked breakfasts; Moira Stuart was far more composed than we were as we sat silently, both wishing we were still in bed, whilst she read out the headlines as we sat in silence.

It's not that I'm particularly bad at getting up. Far from it. Unlike Catherine, I can raise myself out of bed before seven with relative ease. It's just that my brain doesn't start running on all cylinders until at least eight. Before that, I pretty much run on autopilot. Grab coffee, pour cereal into a bowl, shave; that's about as much as I can muster. Wander downstairs to a B&B's dining room and exchange morning communication with the landlady? Not a chance. The B&B's owner could probably tell from the look on our faces that this was going to be a rather quiet breakfast.

She'd kindly arranged for her mother to pop by so that we didn't need to leave the B&B whilst she drove off to wherever the nearest hospital was, but inevitably we about to have an early start. With fifteen miles to do, this was perhaps no bad thing, although we were hardly enthusiastic about it. After stocking up for lunch in Bellingham's small Co-op, we headed on our way.

The Pennine Way signpost at the edge of the town summed up the day ahead. The signpost itself was nothing special in itself. There were many of them like it on the Pennine Way, showing the next major milestone – usually a village or town, but occasionally a summit – with the distance in miles next to it. For most of the signs the distance would be three miles, five miles, whatever. Something to focus on and show progress. Once you got there, you'd find another signpost telling you how far it would be to the next point.

But the sign at Bellingham simply said "Byrness – 14¼". Yes, the next place of any real significance on the Pennine Way would only come once we'd spent all day walking. There was simply nothing of any note in between. We'd be passing through no towns, going near no villages and – although we didn't yet know it – the only soul we'd see would be a forest ranger in his Land Rover.

First order of the day was a climb up a hill, and as we did so we couldn't help but notice that we were walking into cloud. The mist was soon everywhere, giving the moors a rather eerie feeling.

Trees especially. Every now and then, there would be a small clump of them, usually surrounded by a small drystone wall, which would loom out of the cloud; the bare skeletal branches of a tree just coming out of winter, giving everything a rather spooky and ever so slightly sinister feeling.

Remnants of old mines and quarries, the occasional grouse butt, a house hidden behind trees and a completely deserted B6320 road were just some of the sights, but generally there was nothing but heather, tufts of grass and the odd puddle. The rest of the time we could have been anywhere, walking through wilderness. Even the path itself was pretty indistinguishable at times, often looking like it was little more than a sheep trail. Anticipating navigational problems for walkers, the authorities had added a few small signposts at regular intervals, which were just about close enough that in good weather you'd be able to see next one. For us though, it was more "follow what might be a path, and hope for the best."

We somehow made it to the top of Whitley Pike, which, at a height of only 356m, is not exactly one of the Pennine Way's tallest summits. It was at least marked by a small cairn with a wooden post stuck in it, which did give us something to look at. Well, sometimes you have to take your excitement where you can get it. A short way on, we crossed over a small tarmacked track where, next to a cattle grid, someone had put up a sign made out of a square of wood painted white. On it was, simply written, two words. "Thank You." Why? Who knows for nothing else in way of explanation followed.

* * *

The guidebook had optimistically suggested that a good place to stop for lunch could be found a mile or so before Whitley Pike where there was a cairn with a signpost stuck in it. We passed it at half ten, which was just a touch early for the munching of sandwiches. Now, as lunchtime approached, rain started pouring heavily and there was a part of me that really began to wish we had stopped and had a far too early meal break. We did, after all, have an excuse for we had eaten our breakfast much earlier than normal.

What we needed was some shelter, and the forests we that would be walking through in the afternoon did seem to offer the best option. So when we got the top of Padon Hill and saw Redesdale Forest ahead of us, there was the sound of rejoicing. All we had to do was get to the trees.

First though the Pennine Way would require us to spend a couple of miles walking alongside the edge of the forest, and any notion that this was going to be easy walking was quickly discarded when we discovered that to get there required us to walk up what must rank as the worst path on the entire Pennine Way.

The steep uphill path was a complete mudslide, and pretty much unusable. True, we weren't exactly walking the Pennine Way in the finest weather going, but it was hard to imagine this veritable quagmire ever being nice to walk on. There are some paths that, even in the height of a red hot summer, will still be absolute mudbaths. And it didn't take long to realise that this would be one of them.

There was little alternative but to try walking on top of the crumbling remains of a mostly collapsed drystone wall. It was either that or go up to our knees in bog and mud by sticking to the proper. Even the stiles were a nightmare. One was so treacherous looking – all broken, mangled and wet – that I took the decision to brave climbing over a rickety and very pointy barbed wire fence instead.

"This is horrendous," I muttered after spending several minutes just to travel a few metres.

"Yeah," Catherine nodded in agreement. "Sure it will be all right when we get to the top."

Well, you would think so; but the top of Brownrigg Head had other ideas. Whilst everything looked very simple on the map, on the ground the path was almost invisible to see through the matt grass and heather. And for good measure, it was heavily waterlogged. Put your foot in the wrong place and you'd find half your leg would suddenly disappear, quite possibly never to be seen again.

The route the path took was positively torturous, twisting and turning with regular intervals, and its poor condition meant it took us over an hour to walk a mere mile and a half on what the map informed us was flat ground.

On the plus side, we did see a deer lurking

momentarily at the edge of the forest. Which was a great sight, although perhaps nowhere near good enough to make up for the complete torment we had been put through in order to see it.

"It'll be fine when we get into the forest," said Catherine, although I could tell by the look on her face that she wasn't particularly confident that it would be.

And she was right to not be so. What we'd been desperately hoping that we'd join some relatively stable forest track, but instead, as soon as we got into the trees, things got even worse. In our wildest dreams, we couldn't even think that that was even possible but it was, suggesting we probably needed dreams that were just a bit wilder.

A glance at the map showed that we'd be spending the rest of the day in forests. Tallying up revealed we'd done about ten miles already, but still had another five left. If it was all going to be in conditions like this, the going was going to be very tough. We were both hungry, and even though the rain had stopped, there was absolutely nowhere that was even vaguely dry where we could sit down and eat our lunches. And as for sheltering under trees, well that wasn't going to happen as most of them seem to be growing in the middle of sizeable lakes.

We staggered on, tired and frankly rather emotional. And then we came to a gate. And next to the gate was a sign.

Forestry Commission.

Redesdale.
Kielder Forest.
The Forestry Commission welcomes Pennine Way walkers.

A nice greeting. But what was even nicer was that passing through the gate resulted an instant upgrade in path quality. For it turned out there were two sides to Redesdale Forest. The nasty and horrible bit we'd been walking through was a private enterprise which clearly hadn't invested much – if anything – in the quality of its paths and tracks. The Forestry Commission had, on the other hand, built big sturdy ones; ones that were more than capable of surviving a winter onslaught of rain, and that would make walking along oh so much easier. Even better, a check of the map revealed we'd be in Forestry Commission land for the rest of the day. We sighed a huge sigh of relief and even let out a little cheer.

Now there are times on a walk when the thought of walking several miles on stony forest road is not the most appealing prospect in the world. But this was not one of those moments. Given the state of the ground, we had absolutely no desire to leave a track that would keep us dry, and we stuck to it resolutely. We didn't even both following the Pennine Way when it took short-cuts through the trees. The time saved would be counted in minutes, and the waterlogged land may even have made the short cuts taken even longer.

The final piece in the jigsaw puzzle came at half

two, when we finally found a spot we could shelter on the edge of the trees in order to escape the rain and munch on our sandwiches.

As we huddled in the shelter of conifers, a Forestry Commission worker drove by in his van, and decided to stop and say hello.

"There's snow forecast tonight," he said as we chatted away. "No idea how bad it's going to be, but it's going to come down."

We nodded. We'd seen the forecast ourselves, although had tried our best to ignore it. The forecast had started saying there would be a couple of small snow showers, but as the days had progressed the amount of snow predicted seemed to be increasing dramatically. But what could we do, other than hope for the best.

Bidding him farewell, we set off for the few remaining miles that would take us to Byrness; the final stretch providing little more challenging than a damp path and a ford of a heavily swollen river. We arrived on the edge of the village next to a small stone church, a hotel and a boarded up petrol station with signs inaccurately informing drivers that it was the last place to fill up before Scotland.

The rest of Byrness lay a short way down the A86, down which cars and lorries thundered along. Much of the village was originally built in the 1930s by the Forestry Commission to house the army of workers required to maintain its new plantations in the area. Over the years, changes in forestry practises meant that fewer staff were needed and the houses began to be sold off to private owners, two of which were converted by the YHA into a youth hostel for Pennine Way walkers.

For many years the place had a dire reputation, with a rating of a mere single star. In an old copy of the Pennine Way Association newsletter we'd seen, one correspondent had charitably proclaimed "no-one I know has ever eulogised about Byrness hostel, it really is rather basic." But with the nearby hotel only having three bedrooms, there wasn't much choice for many. The nearest alternative accommodation was many miles away, with no easy way to get there. There was certainly no point pressing on and going further along the Pennine Way. The trail wouldn't go near another village for another twenty-six miles. The hostel may have been dire, but at least it was there.

And then in 2006 the YHA decided to get out and put the two cottages on the market. It was part of a massive program that saw 17 hostels under threat of closure, six of which were on the Pennine Way.

The other five hostels were all in areas where there was a reasonable amount of alternative accommodation, but in Byrness the closure would have been a complete disaster for Pennine Way walkers in a part of the world where facilities were already sparse. Byrness had no shop, no pub, the local GP had closed, as had the village school. The petrol station had gone, the local milkman had retired and the only public transport connections was a daily National Express coach and a daily local bus service.

Thankfully though, along with four other threatened Pennine Way hostels, Byrness was saved. It was sold to new owners Colin and Joyce who had a plan to completely upgrade the place, and boost the place up the accommodation ratings as far as possible.   Whilst remaining a YHA franchise, the the hostel was completely renovated and redecorated, and re-opened under the new name of Forest View. And as Colin showed us round, there was clearly pride in what they'd achieved, with particular focus on the much needed drying room which was heated by a shiny new biomass boiler.

"We've also got a small shop for supplies," Colin added as it took us towards the lounge. "And our famous beer cupboard."

A key was whisked out and inserted into a small hole in the wood, and within seconds doors were thrown back to reveal a cupboard absolutely jam packed with beer and wine. Most of it consisted of bottled ales, providing a choice that was frankly far, far larger than the average pub.

"We've had people taking photographs of it and posting them on the internet!" he added.

What could I say? I was tempted to take a photograph of it myself.

"You know there's snow forecast?" he added, changing the subject.

We nodded grimly, although slightly assured that whatever did happen, we would be fine on the alcohol front.

***

There was a fire roaring away in the dining room, and we settled into its warm embrace. Pretty much everything we'd been wearing had been drenched by the time we'd got to Forest View, and after a miserable day we gladly settled down for a much needed hot meal, followed by attempts to make a (slight) dent in Colin's beer supplies. But there was a hint of uneasiness as we headed back to our room to settle down for the night.

It wasn't to be the best nights sleep. With no TV or radio, we'd had to resort to using the patchy mobile signal in order to get some information on the state of play. As the evening had gone on, the forecasts had changed. There were now weather warnings in force. Severe ones.

Looking out of the window revealed little sign that anything was likely to happen. Just the ever present cloud and a little rain. Everything just looked completely normal.

As our heads wearily hit our pillows, we knew all we could do was simply wait and see what the morning brought us.

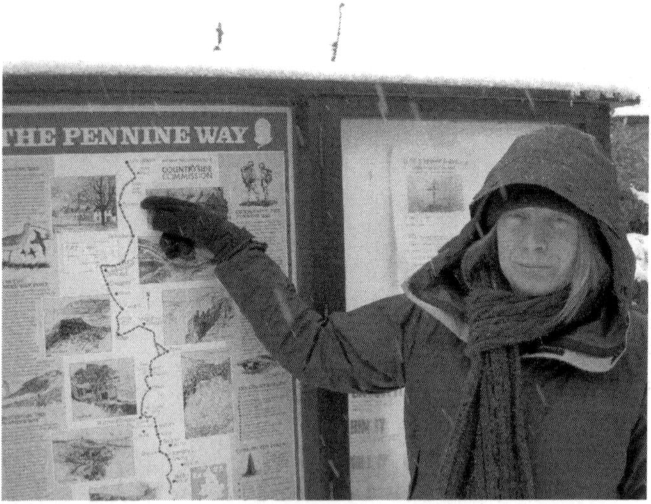
THE PENNINE WAY
COUNTRYSIDE COMMISSION

Stuck in Byrness

The next morning I woke and hesitantly opened the curtains to see what awaited us.

"What's it like out there?" asked Catherine, waking up as the light filled the room.

"White," I replied, glumly. "Very, very white."

Snow was coming down heavily, and Forest View's small garden was deeply coated in the stuff already.

Downstairs we pottered around, preparing breakfast and wondering what on earth to do. Kirk Yetholm lay 26 miles away. We'd intended to walk it in two sections, stopping overnight at a remote farm along the way. But to get there would require us to head up onto high ground. To compound matters, the hills didn't provide the best conditions even in good weather. The previous night, one of Forest View's other residents had told us she'd been up on the hills where the Pennine Way went the day before and had put a foot wrong and ended up to her waist in bog. Now that same section of path was covered in snow, and who knew how much of it was up there.

Even without the potential problems caused by deep bog being hidden under a heavy coating of the white stuff, navigation would be extremely difficult, and we certainly weren't equipped or experienced enough to walk in such conditions. True, we were assuming that everywhere would be bad. We had absolutely no idea what it was like outside Byrness. It could all be fine a mile away. Stranger things have happened, although it seemed highly unlikely. If Byrness was cut off, chances were that the higher ground would be even worse.

As we dawdled around wondering what to do, Colin arrived to tell us that the roads were pretty much closed; the busy A86 had ground to a halt and would remain so until the snow ploughs managed to get through.

And then the phone calls started.

The first was for two women, fellow Forest View residents who had been planning to drive some forty miles to the remote Mounthooley bunkhouse. Roads were impassible, proclaimed the owner over the phone.

Then a few minutes later, the owners of our B&B at Barrowburn Farm were on the line.

"You're best not even trying to get here," was their comment. "We're completely snowed in. It's very deep."

Well, that was that then. That just left the question of what on earth we were going to do now.

The snow ploughs arrived by mid-morning, and whilst the snow was easing a little, it was still coming down. The hostel's four other residents – two women, and a man and a woman – decided to brave the roads as best they could, but for us there were few options. To say that the chances that the daily bus and coach services would be running were pretty slim, was an understatement. There was little choice. There was no way round it; we were stopping at Byrness another night.

According to our original itinerary, the following night would see us stay at the youth hostel in Kirk Yetholm. Obviously given the snow, there would have been little reason to actually head there. But as it happened, we had plans. Waiting for us at Kirk Yetholm would be Catherine's parents, her brother and his wife. A table was booked for us all at the Border Inn that evening. A table booked for a dual celebration. We'd toast our success in finally completing the Pennine Way, and we'd also raise a glass to celebrate Catherine's mum's 60th birthday and her completion of Ben Nevis. True, there'd be nothing to celebrate about the Pennine Way, but it has to be said that birthdays generally are generally not affected by the weather.

Really, there weren't many options. It was Kirk Yetholm or bust. But it certainly wasn't going to be Kirk Yetholm by foot. We'd have to make separate arrangements.

As it happened, Colin and Joyce needed to get to the town of Kelso the following morning, and they were confident the roads would be clear enough for them to get down there and – most importantly – get back home too. And for us, we'd be able to get the bus to Kirk Yetholm, and the pub, meaning we'd be able to meet everyone.

But that was tomorrow. Today we'd be in Byrness, and as the snow continued to fall, we sought a way to occupy ourselves.

As Colin bustled around doing his morning

chores, and with the snow continuing to come down heavily, we could think of little to do other than sit in the hostel playing games. We'd brought with us a German card game called Bohnanza, which kept us occupied for a bit, but after an hour or so we started raiding the hostel's small game selection. This include Scrabble and a thrilling game known as Farmyard Donkey which proved so tedious that only the knowledge that there were many hours of the day remaining before we could go to bed, kept us playing it.

By lunchtime we were thoroughly sick of cards of any form, but as luck would have it, the flurry of snow falling had reduced to merely a light snow shower. Feeling thoroughly cooped up, we headed pulled on our still slightly damp hiking boots, and headed outside.

There were a couple of simple looking circular walks in the forest, accessible from the Pennine Way. It wasn't quite the fifteen miles we'd anticipated doing, but it was better than nothing.

Daffodils drooped their heads in the grounds of the village church; a reminder that this was nearly the end of March. A sign at the front of the church announced it was one of the smallest in Northumberland.

The world was in monochrome; the bright snow set against the darkness of pretty much everything else. Up ahead we could see the low clouds hogging the hillside. Visibility on the Pennine Way would undoubtedly be poor, and that was before you even considered the fact that the paths would be impossible to see.

We wandered on back to the Kielder Forest. It was deserted. Everywhere was deserted. The few people in the area were all no doubt safely tucked up indoors, probably sat in front of roaring fires. The roads were still in poor condition, with just a handful of vehicles doing their best to get through to wherever they were going. There was a caravan park nearby. Someone of them even had awnings erected. But if there was anyone staying there, they weren't providing much sign of it.

We potted around as long as we could, before deciding that this was all too cold for us, and headed back to Forest View for a cup of tea, and many, many games of Scrabble.

* * *

The next morning was the first of April. The sun was shining brightly; the sky a bold blue. Perfect walking weather; the kind we'd been hoping for ever since we'd arrived at Dufton several days earlier. But sadly we weren't going to Kirk Yetholm on foot today.

As Colin and Joyce drove us out of Byrness and over the border into Scotland, we looked out of the car windows at the world around us. The higher ground was still covered in snow, but as the road began to descend to the valley, it was completely notable by its absence. The towns and villages we passed through looked like they hadn't had a single drop of the stuff.

We potted around the town of Kelso for a bit, admiring the ruined abbey buildings from afar as the abbey site was closed. Apparently it opened in April. Well this was April – the first of the month – but the place was having none of it. A trip to Floors Castle, built by the 1st Duke of Roxburghe in 1721, was another option but as we got there a sign informed us that it too was closed. If we wanted to visit, we'd have to pop back the following day. With several hours to kill, and the town's two main tourist attractions firmly closed, we ended up doing a self-guided walking tour of the town, based on Scottish playwright and novelist Walter Scott and his connections with the town. This included such landmarks as the site of a tree which once inspired Scott. The tree was no longer there, having disappeared several years earlier.

After some food in a café, which seemed to have an extensive sideline in dubious looking CDs and VHS tapes of Scottish folk songs played on the bagpipes by a rotund man in a kilt, we decided we'd exhausted Kelso's possibilities and headed to the main square to catch the bus to Kirk Yetholm.

After a short journey, the bus pulled up outside the Border Hotel, next to the official finishing point of the Pennine Way. We'd made it then, just not under our own steam. We were still a little too early to check into the hostel, we wandered up the Pennine Way a little to see the hills we should have been walking over.

It didn't take us long for the Cheviots to come into sight. There they were, covered heavily in a blanket of white snow. We stared at them, feeling a sense of defeat.

"We'll have to come back then," I said, finally.

"We will. Perhaps when the weather's a little better?" replied Catherine.

"Yep. That might just be a good idea."

And with that, we turned round, and headed back to the village to party.

Part 5

Byrness to Kirk Yetholm
Fifth trip walking the Pennine Way

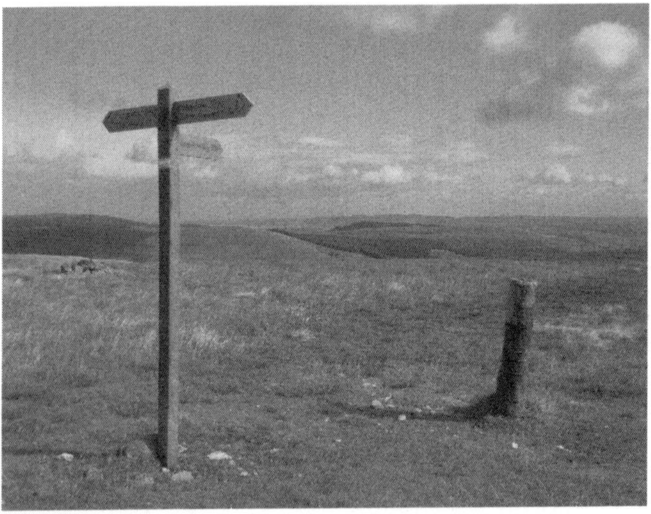

Byrness to Windy Gyle

"So you folks heading to Byrness then?" asked the driver as we boarded the National Express coach that was stood in the coach terminal at Newcastle.

His thick Mersey twang suggested the driver and his passengers had already come quite a distance. Most of them were heading to Edinburgh, and the tone of his voice suggested that those that alighted at Byrness were few and far between. Indeed, as we raced through the Northumbrian countryside, the coach doors didn't open once until it had pulled up an hour later to let us off.

That Byrness is on the National Express network at all is nothing short of a miracle. It is, after all, a tiny community in the middle of absolutely nowhere. Completely surrounded by forests, it is not the obvious calling stop for an intercity public transport service.

It only gets its service because the village sits just off the main road to the far larger town of Jedburgh; a place that is slightly more deserving of its coach link. Deserving enough anyway for the coach company to justify running one coach a day through it in each direction. The coach even gets a bit of competition on its journey, in the form of a local bus service which also runs once a day, a few hours earlier.

Not surprisingly, we were the only ones to alight in the village, or more accurately, alight outside the deserted and still firmly closed petrol station on the edge of Byrness.

Six months after being snowed in there, we were finally back to finally complete the Pennine Way. Or at least, we hoped.

As soon as we'd arrived back home after our abortive trip, the diaries had come out whilst we tried to work out just when we'd be able to get back again. It would not be easiest of jaunts. Such is the remoteness of Byrness that it can take almost a whole day just to get there, and getting back to London from Kirk Yetholm isn't much easier. It was a lot of travelling for a mere two days on the hills.

In the end we settled on the August bank holiday. I was going to be in the north of England anyway, having spent a week walking the Dales Way to Windermere. A mere three trains would take me to Newcastle where I'd meet Catherine fresh off her train from London. Ironically, her journey would be slightly quicker than my own.

Byrness was in blazing sunshine – a far cry from the state we'd left it in. We wandered towards the hostel, seeing the village in a whole new light. True, the petrol station was still closed, but on the other side, the hotel had opened up a café. And down at Forest View, the beer cupboard seemed to be groaning even more under the weight of the bottles. But most importantly, it looked like we really were finally going to finish the Pennine Way, and there would be little that could stop us.

* * *

The next morning we heaved our packs on our backs and headed off to do the steep but steady climb out of the forest, and on to the top of Byrness Hill. On a clear day the hill provides the walker with a fine view of the forested landscape below; a sweeping panoramic including the previous days' route.

Looking back is in some respects preferable, for this outstanding scenery is, rather perversely, blighted. Here is another case of land being under military control, as the hill leads on to the Ottorburn Ranges, which are owned and used by the Army for training purposes. Indeed, the Ministry of Defence owns 20% of the land in the Northumberland National Park. Thankfully live bullets are no longer used in the area, however the concept that a National Park – a place established to conserve a beautiful environment – can be scarred by military use seems rather wrong to me.

Still, that was the least of our worries, as a rather fine path soon degenerated into one of the Pennine Way's trademarks: peat bog.

By this stage we'd walked over our fair share of the Pennine Way's most defining feature. Many an old picture of Pennine Way walkers in the 1960s and 1970s shows people leaping over giant peat groughs, or squelching through muddy morasses. In Earby Youth Hostel we'd found an entire photo album of them. With modern eyes though, it's hard to imagine. In at attempt to prevent erosion in the fragile landscape, many sections of the Pennine Way have now been paved over with large stone slabs; so much so that sometimes if you had your eyes closed, and didn't know where you were, you might well think you were just walking down the shops for a pint of milk. Well, until you put your foot down in the wrong place, and find that to the side of the flagstone is a huge muddy puddle.

The paving, however, is usually concentrated on the most popular walking areas, and the further north the trail goes, the more sporadic the stone flags and board-walks get. And there are some places you come to where you think the flags really should be there, but aren't. And there were few places that fitted the bill more than the delightfully named Ravens Knowe where even the sunshine couldn't disguise a wet, muddy quagmire of a path.

As Catherine went wide – very, very wide – round in an attempt to escape the worst of it, I opted to bounce from grassy hummock to grassy hummock, in an attempt to spend as little time on the ground as I could. This went amazingly well until I realised that I'd run out of hummocks. I stood on the final one, assessing the situation. Most of the ground in front of me was bog, but there was one patch that looked like it was dry enough to stand on; a barren-looking piece of earth in an otherwise soggy quagmire. But putting my best foot forward I was greeted with a distinct case of that sinking feeling. Literally. Before I knew it, both my feet were being sucked down into the ground, and they were doing it fast.

"Hang on! Hang on!" shouted Catherine, spotting my predicament from her location of safety which seemed to be several miles away, whilst I stood static in fear.

Now I've (so far) never been stuck in quicksand however I have a suspicion it shares some similarities with the bog I was now stuck in. My first attempt to struggle out only saw me sink down further and faster, and soon I was up to my waist in it with absolutely no idea how to get out. There was nothing to push against with my feet, just more dank smelling ooze, so that ruled that out. Catherine was busy shouting at me that she was coming, whilst simultaneously being thwarted in her attempts by other large sections of bog. Not wanting her to be trapped too, I tried to get her to stay away whilst I desperately worked out what on earth I was going to do.

Truth be told, I've no real idea how I actually got out. I couldn't even minutes after it happened. It was just all a blur. I think I had a kind of feeling that leaning forward would help. Indeed, doing so would have distributed my weight more widely over the bog, thus reducing the chance of me sinking; knowledge which just goes to show that my GCSE in Physics has indeed had at least one practical application in the years since I was at school. For years I'd considered the knowledge that someone walking in a stiletto heel would do more than damage to a polished floor, than a full size elephant doing the same, to be distinctly useless. Now those same principles may have just saved my bacon.

As well as leaning forward, I've an image of pulling myself forward out of the bog, although frankly I've no idea what I used to lever myself on that pull. But somehow I managed it and stood there, half my body soaked and covered in peat bog, feeling rather cold.

"Is the camera all right" asked the love of my life who'd had finally made it over to me from her hundred mile diversion and now that she had, was determined to show her most caring side.

* * *

They say that the grass is greener on the other side, and having ascertained that the camera was, indeed, all right, I decided to test out that hypothesis.

Much of the journey between Byrness and Kirk Yetholm is spent following a fence that marks the border between Scotland and England. The path spends most of its time on the English side, but occasionally decides it fancies a change and pops over into Scotland. As I looked over the fence into Scotland, I noticed that the ground looked far more stable over there. Did this line of wire and fence posts have some magical properties? Or was it just because no one ever walked on the Scottish side because the path was on the other? Who cared? In an attempt to avoid finding myself falling in any more bog, I hopped over the fence and strolled along happily and in safety.

It was soon necessary to return to England, however the worst was over as the path now became paved. Even so, the paving isn't guaranteed to protect the walker from all the worst that the hills can offer as I found out a mere half hour later. Having finally dried out from my dunking, I was happily admiring the view as I walked, meaning I failed to notice several planks were missing from the board-walk I was on. The result being that I promptly put my foot down in to a deep pool of very cold water.

* * *

Chew Green is the site of a Roman Camp and Fortlet, although the few remains and earthworks are now mostly colonised by sheep who watched with vague interest as I took the opportunity to sit down on some dry land and wring out my sodden socks. They might have even wondered why I was wearing thin trainer socks rather than the stiff walking socks. I confess I found myself wondering the exact same thing myself.

There had been a strong wind blowing since we'd got up on the ridge, and the blue skies from earlier the day had been blown off to somewhere else. In their place, grey clouds with an ominous look about them had arrived and no sooner had we struggled in to our waterproofs, the showers began. Ah, this was more like the Pennine Way I knew and loved.

The wind and rain whipped our faces in a most

delightful way; every drop stinging against our cheeks. It was a delight to finally make it to the mountain rescue hut at Yearning Saddle where we could at least shelter from the elements and have some lunch.

"Cold out!" came a voice as we opened the door to find we were not the only ones seeking respite from the weather.

The hut was pretty crowded with of fellow walkers. True there were only six of us in total, however it was a small hut. We stepped inside to join a couple who were out doing a circular walk, and a retired couple called Philip and Jean who were two fellow Pennine Way walkers that we'd chatted to earlier in the morning outside of Byrness. As we munched and lunched, the wind battered and howled against the sturdy wooden building, although slowly but surely, the rain stopped and the blue skies began to slowly re-appear. The wind, however, was with us to stay.

As is customary we perused the shelter's log book, which was full of moans and groans about the horrendous weather conditions. All except one who'd scrawled: "I don't know what everyone's complaining about, I came in here to shelter from the sun!"

Being the last ones entering, we were also the last ones out when we finally stepped out of the hut once more and headed on along Lamb Hill before climbing up the endearingly named Beefstand Hill, which gave us our first view of the mighty Cheviot, which, along with a range of hills named in its honour, dominates the landscape.

Strange names seemed to be a feature of the area as we marched on over Mozie Law and Plea Know, although the names aren't what the area is best known for. In fact, it's distinctive for the herd of wild goats that roam the landscape, which we caught a glimpse of in the distance. Where they came from, no one really knows. How long they've been there, no one is particularly sure. About all that is known is that they've been resident on the Cheviot hills for centuries.

* * *

These days, the word "gyle" is a term related to the brewing of stout or ale; a word added to our language courtesy of the Dutch where it is derived from a word meaning "to boil, ferment."

Quite what it means in the context of the place name Windy Gyle, is another question entirely. It seemed unlikely that some ancient predecessor of Arthur Guinness popped up here with a mash tun and started brewing pints for the thirsty goats. The first part of Windy Gyle's name was certainly true though. If we'd thought that the breezes were a tad on the stiff side earlier, it was nothing to the battering we got as we tried to take in the panoramic views from the summit.

The summit itself was a large pile of rocks known as Russell's Cairn, on which someone had ceremoniously plonked a trig point, which at least provided a something to hold on to as we struggled to stay upright in the face of the wind. And no, Russell wasn't a brewer either. The cairn itself is a Bronze Age burial cairn, although its name is newer; named after Lord Francis Russell who was murdered nearby in 1585.

For centuries the border country was a place of lawlessness. Clans and families would frequently switch allegiances between the English and Scottish crowns based on what suited their own interests at the time, meaning that neither monarch's will was particularly headed. And then there were the border reivers; bandits and thieves who would raid farms and steal from the residents.

An attempt had been made in the 13th century to establish a kind of buffer zone, splitting the area into six "Marches" – three on each side of the border – which would be run by Wardens who were given the unenviable task of trying to keep the peace, and enforce the law. At regular intervals the wardens would all meet at isolated spots along the border to agree tactics and co-ordinate their efforts; places such as Windy Gyle. It was at one such meeting that Lord Francis Russell – a former warden himself and a senior politician – was murdered.

As well as marking history, the cairn also marked the spot where we would leave the Pennine Way for the day for a long detour to our accommodation.

With no road access or habitations in the area, Byrness to Kirk Yetholm is one of the trickiest sections of the Pennine Way to organise a bed for the night. Some hardy souls opt to camp, or bivvy down at one of the two mountain rescue huts. Others even attempt to do the whole 27 miles in one day. But most walkers make arrangements with their accommodation providers in Kirk Yetholm or Byrness, who – usually for a small fee – will pick you up at an arranged point a few miles down in the valley.

For me though, one of the joys of long distance walking is moving from one place to another each day. You leave one village or town in the morning, then end up somewhere completely different in the evening. The thought of going back to somewhere you've just come from, or indeed getting to the next place a day early, well it just feels wrong. But thankfully we'd tracked down an alternative. For deep in the valley below was a remote farmhouse B&B.

One of the most famous farmhouse B&Bs on the Pennine Way was Uswayford Farm, however its owners had retired in 2009; a fact I had found after I'd headed onto the internet in search of answers after repeated phone calls went unanswered. It turned out that the new owners had abruptly left following a harsh winter that they were completely unprepared for. They'd even planned to do B&B and had taken several bookings, leaving some Pennine Way walkers turning up and finding themselves looking at an empty house. Although someone was presumably still paying the phone bills.

Thankfully though, we'd found an alternative for

a few miles along in the Coquet Valley, lies Barrowburn Farm with its tea room, camping barn, and B&B. The one problem was that it was a three mile diversion to get there, mostly following the Border Country Ride bridleway. But at least it was downhill and we headed down in to the valley, gradually losing height and passing by more forests and the intriguingly named Murder Cleugh, which curiously included a small tombstone, engraved with the text:

> Murder Cleugh
> Here in 1610 Robert Lumsden killed Isabella Sudden

The memorial, we later found out, was created by a local resident who was a local history expert with masonry skills. In an attempt to ensure that local history was nor forgotten, he went round erecting several such markers in the area.

A spectacular rainbow welcomed us as we got close to our destination. A huge arc, it was one of the biggest and finest I'd ever seen, with both ends fully visible. Was there a pot of gold at one of the ends? No there wasn't, but one of them did seem to coincide with Barrowburn farm where we were promptly welcomed with a cup of tea and a cheese scone.

Starkly furnished with bare floors, and a rather old looking bathroom with a hot water tap that spluttered enthusiastically as it dispensed its wares, Barrowburn perhaps wasn't the most glamorous

B&B to stay in, however the welcome was warm, and the views out of its windows were fine.

I'd never stayed somewhere so remote. Besides the smattering of farm buildings, a phone box and a road, there was absolutely nothing for miles around. Just big skies and big hills. As we ate our evening meal I was almost hypnotised by the stunning sight of clouds sailing through the valley.

With most walkers safely tucked up in the comfort of the Border Hotel in Kirk Yetholm, or raiding Byrness hostel's beer cupboard, I knew where I wanted to be. This was perhaps the finest view we'd seen all day, and one that most Pennine Way walkers would never see.

We were lucky. Very lucky indeed.

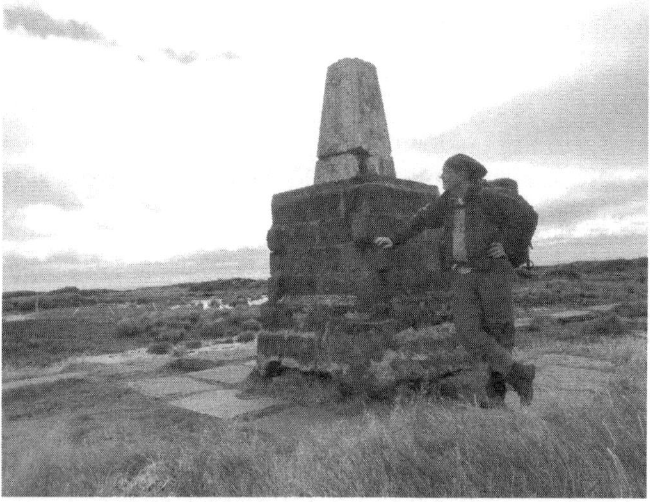

Windy Gyle to Kirk Yetholm

"Now I've got a bit of a proposition for you," said Ian – one of the couple who ran Barrowburn – with a look on his face that some people would use if they were about to suggest that we all popped to the nearest patisserie and each eat three chocolate éclairs there and then. In reality he was offering us a lift part of the way back to the Pennine Way, which for some walkers would equate to the same thing.

"Yesterday you got here by coming down the Border Country Ride, didn't you?"

We nodded to say we did.

"Now we can drop you off on that bit, or we can take you a bit further on and you can walk up Clennell Street instead. You'll get up on the ridge about half a mile on from Windy Gyle. It's entirely up to you. Some people don't feel right about missing a bit. But you've got to walk a bit anyway to get back from here."

Very true indeed. Either way, even after kind offer of a lift, we'd still need to walk a mile and a half walk up hill before we'd get back to the Pennine Way; there was simply no way to get closer by car.

"And you'll be able to see Windy Gyle from where Clennell Street takes you"

Ah well. Now that he put it like that, well let's just say that it clinched the deal.

Some people may, at this point, talk about respecting the integrity of the walk – that the Pennine Way walker should do every inch of its route if they wish to claim they'd done the whole thing. But then we'd got lost and gone wrong on the very first day we'd set foot on the Pennine Way, and on one summit we made a substantially wrong turning that had resulted in us ending up several miles further down a valley than we should have been. Right near the end was probably not the place to suddenly start getting obsessive about covering the whole of the Pennine Way with 100% accuracy.

As we ate a hearty breakfast, I struggled to really believe that this would be the last day we'd spend walking the Pennine Way. After it being a part of our life for over three years, we were almost done. And best of all, it looked like it was going to be a fantastic day to complete it. As we headed up the ancient drovers road of Clennell Street, the sun was shining brightly and the winds calm. This was perfect walking weather on which to end our Pennine Way adventure, and so unlike most of the walking days we'd had so far.

Having done most of the trail in spring and autumn, the weather hadn't generally been on our side. But here we were, walking on August Bank Holiday Monday, basking in the sunshine. As we arrived back on the ridge we looked back to Windy Gyle where we'd been the previous day and saw the amazing sight of its trig point shimmering. Just shimmering. It would have been hard to ask for more.

* * *

It was gone eleven by the time we'd finally rejoined the Pennine Way, rejoining another row of paving slabs over the heather topped ground.

Despite it being a Bank Holiday, there was no one around. Only months later did I remember that it was only a holiday in England, due to Scotland having their August bank holiday at the beginning of the month, rather than the end. This also wasn't the most populated part of the world, however I expected to see more people than just the two fellow walkers we spotted in the distance who were joined by their enthusiastic dogs who bounded over the tufts of heather with glee.

After a short rest, we walked on over the slabs that covered Butt Roads and King's Seat. In the distance we could just make out the Hanging Stone whose macabre name make it sound more impressive than it actually looks. The name is said to have been given when a packman's pack slipped over the edge of the rock; the strap going tight around his neck.

Just beyond we came to a three armed signpost, each arm rather oddly informing us that the Pennine Way went in every direction it was pointing. This slightly confusing state of affairs was because we'd reached the optional detour to the rectangular, almost boxy summit of the Cheviot. Whilst not a compulsory part of the Pennine Way, the majority of Pennine Way walkers do decide that they haven't walked anywhere near enough on their trip, so head off to make the two mile round trip to visit the final major peak on the trail.

Of those that make it, few ever seem to have a good word about the place. They will tell you that it's a dull, boring peat bog quagmire with few, if any, redeeming features to justify the detour. As Wainwright summed it up,

> "most walkers will arrive at the west top of Cairn Hill, where the detour starts, already tired, and will, if favoured by survival and after due passage of valuable time return to the said west top of Cairn Hill none the richer."

For many a Pennine Way walker recalling their experience, the trip up the top of the Cheviot would have been a dull journey, battling through the stale smelling bog water; boots covered in peat. You don't even get a view when you finally make it to the top as the summit is a plateau. And as it's the highest point for miles around, there's little that can be seen. It's probably not even worth taking your camera out of your bag because there will be little worthy of a photograph. Besides, you might drop your camera in a bog and never see it again. Some have measured the peat bog on the Cheviot to be up to two metres in depth. This is certainly not somewhere you'd want to lose your camera by any means.

Common sense and reason said there was no

point in going. But despite it, sometimes you just have to. Don't you?

Thankfully these days accessing the top of the Cheviot is a bit easier thanks to a row of stone slabs that snake their way over the ground. The main challenge is merely a case of walking from one to the another, trying to avoid inexplicably losing our balance, lest we landed head first in the black stuff.

As we headed up to the top, the hill seemed to come to life. All of a sudden, voices with distinct Geordie twangs filled the air, and there were people everywhere. Well, on the paving stones anyway. Other paths joined ours, and soon we were part of a a steady stream of people heading up to the Cheviot; a sizeable proportion of the population of the North East seemed to be making the most of their bank holiday by paying it a visit.

Sitting at the summit, sheltering under the trig point that had been plonked on a large stone tableau, more and more walkers continued to appear, most using the paths, but one woman began to bound enthusiastically over what appeared to be some horrendous peat bog, heading for goodness knows where.

Shaking our heads at her reckless abandon, we headed back from whence we came, now joined by a middle aged man wearing a Newcastle United shirt and a woolly hat.

"I wanna see the Hangin' Stone" he told us in a thick Geordie accent, looking all around him just in case he missed it. "It's on me map somewhere round here."

"Yeah, we saw it earlier. Doesn't look much."

"Oh well, it's on me map! I'm lookin' forward to seein' it!"

Quite what he spoke about in that half hour that he managed to spend with us, I can't honestly tell you. What I do know is that we barely got two words in. There was just a constant stream of words coming from his mouth. Somehow he managed to talk both non-stop, and nineteen to the dozen at exactly the same time. It was a feat that took quite a lot of skill, and I can't believe I've ever heard anyone say so many words in so little time ever before in my life. It was so constant that Catherine and myself ended up walking in some sort of daze; a situation that continued until we passed Philip, one half of the retired couple we'd seen the day before. He was heading up to the Cheviot solo as Jean, his wife, had sensibly decided to skip it and have a rest at the turn off not far below.

The day before we'd found out that we were staying at the same B&B in Kirk Yetholm as Philip and Jean, although they were staying there for two nights. We had a quick chat with him whilst our new Geordie friend remained strangely silent; his desire to see the hanging stone perhaps not as strong as his desire to be around other people.

We left Philip to continue his quest to the top of the Cheviot, and set on again for the main path, knowing that here at least, we'd be able to leave our loquacious new friend behind. The hanging stone was back where we had already been, and if our

Geordie friend continued walking with us, he'd be going nowhere near where he wanted to go. We would be free! On the other hand, someone else probably was going to suffer, and as we approached the crossroads we knew who that person probably would be. Jean was stood there, resting against a fencepost. Her fate was sealed, and there was little chance she'd be able to escape.

We shot her an apologetic look as we bade our farewells, knowing that chances were that she'd be stuck in a one-way conversation for at least half an hour until Philip returned from the Cheviot. We later learned that that was exactly what had happened, until he finally headed off on his own to complete his quest. Whether he did finally make it to the stone, and what he made it when it got there, we never did find out.

* * *

Auchope Cairn didn't get a particularly glowing write up in out guide book. "[It] must be the most exposed and uncomfortable place on the whole ridge" the author commented. "There is a small stone shelter which provides some protection from the wind, but it is a better idea to descend by the north-west path and make for the more complete shelter provided by a mountain rescue hut."

Based on that recommendation, it didn't seem a particularly obvious spot to stop for lunch, although Catherine was having none of it as she extolled the virtues of the views of hills and valleys that were presented in front of us. The mountain rescue hut would be dark and we wouldn't be able to see much, she had said. Besides, it's a nice day. How could the cairn really be that bad?

As we began to unwrap our sandwiches, that question was swiftly answered as a strong wind appeared suddenly out of nowhere, and started battering us. Suddenly sitting in front of a great view was not quite so appealing, and it wasn't long before we were finishing up and scurrying off down the path towards Auchope Shelter.

Dropping down a few hundred metres in height certainly helped keep us warmer, but it also a symbolic descent. Although we still had a few hills to climb, our general trend was now downwards. There was just one last big hill to tackle first. The rocky summit of the Schil sits on the border, and we were still on the England side. Sitting at the top, we looked back at the ridge we'd followed for the last two days, and admired the Cheviot in front of us as much you can for a rather boxy hill.

It would all soon be over. Not far off the Schil's summit we made the last crossing into Scotland and followed the path slowly but surely to Kirk Yetholm. The hills began to fall away, replaced by fields and pasture. Farming was the order of the day now, shown at the bottom of Latchly Hill, as we were slowed down by sheep being herded in to a field. We joined a small country lane that would take us gently to the end of the trail, occasionally looking back to see what we'd left behind.

In our abortive trip a few months before, we'd

made it to Kirk Yetholm in the end, only by bus. On that bright and sunny April morning, I'd stood where we stood now, looking at those same hills, then covered in snow, wondering what we'd missed. Now we knew.

Before we knew it, we were standing outside the Border Hotel; the finishing point just outside. Posing for the obligatory celebratory photographs, we headed to the B&B to dump our stuff and freshen up before celebrating in style.

* * *

In 1968 Alfred Wainwright walked the Pennine Way in order to write his book, The Pennine Way Companion. For most of his travels the weather was appalling which must have contributed to his rather negative view of the whole endeavour. He was so unimpressed with what he saw that he made arrangements for those who finished the walk, to receive a free pint in the Border Hotel. By 1979 this was reduced to a half pint, but Wainwright continued picking up the tab, even leaving money in his will to cover the costs. It cost an estimated £15,000 during his life, and although his money has long run out, the tradition continues to this day, now sponsored by a local brewery.

What the exact criteria are for claiming it, we never asked. Having not walked the whole thing in one go we didn't feel right taking up the offer, although you could argue doing it over three years takes far more commitment than someone doing it in just three weeks. Still, we paid for our own, although doffed our caps to the picture of Wainwright which hung at the end of the bar, as we supped and read the contents of the pub's Pennine Way signing in book.

If three years felt like a long time to do the route, that was nothing compared to some others. Reading through the book revealed that one walker had taken seventeen years to complete it. Woes were common. One woman had even lost her camera to bog. I'd had the worry that it would happen to me several times, although thankfully it always escaped.

But the best comment came from Bob Griffiths. It simply said "Big hills. Big rain. Big smile." We nodded in agreement to that, and got another pint in.

* * *

When we'd made the booking, the owner of our B&B (who, in one of those weird twists that life throws at you, had once lived a mile or so from our house in London) had been most keen to ensure we had a table booked at the pub for our evening meal, even if it was a Monday. And whilst out in the hills, we'd learned that one had been booked for us.

The message was relayed to us by Philip and Jean, when we'd met them earlier. It was a slightly confusing message. We knew the B&B owners had booked a table for us all, but we didn't quite know whether that they'd booked two tables for two, or one for four.

On arrival at the B&B we found out that it had been a table for four that had been booked, although we didn't quite get why, nor whether Philip and Jean were expecting that either. Having a meal with two random strangers wasn't something we were particularly used to but being too polite, we had just decided to sit around the pub until they arrived and see what they did. If they turned up and went "Oh, we're all together are we?!" in a confused way, we'd work something out.

They didn't. And within minutes I began to suspect it had been Philip's idea all along. A retired teacher, he was a happy and very chatty bloke, although thankfully not in the same way as the lone Geordie we'd encountered earlier.

Between the pair of them, Philip and Jean had walked most of the major walking routes in the country, from the Coast to Coast, to the Thames Path. But what most struck me from their conversation was their comment about just how few people they'd seen walking the Pennine Way.

Being the granddaddy of UK walking routes and the one everyone knows, I've always had this image of the Pennine Way as being a busy route. Admittedly we had seen few walking it on our many travels, however we'd put that down to the fact that we'd been walking it at odd points of the year, rather than in summer when most people would be doing it.

Philip and Jean however had walked the whole thing in August, right at the peak of the walking calendar. And in that whole time they'd managed to see eight others walking it. And that included the two of us. Even the signing in books had looked sparse to us when we'd viewed them.

We chatted away about anything and everything; us all sharing our experiences and looking back at what we'd done. And we had done it. Our names were there, bold as brass, in the Border Hotel's signing in book. As they were in those of the Pen-y-Ghent Café many miles – and for that matter, some years – earlier. Back at a point when we hadn't even realised we would be walking the whole thing.

As we headed back to London the next day, battling with a real world of delayed trains and signalling problems at York, it felt like there was now something missing. It had been with us for three years of our lives, and now there was a gap. A 267 mile Pennine Way shaped hole. Strange as it seems, I was missing it already.

Sighing, I knew what that meant. It was going to happen. Someday I'd end up doing it all over again. All I could do was hope that I wouldn't end up up to my waist in bog the next time.

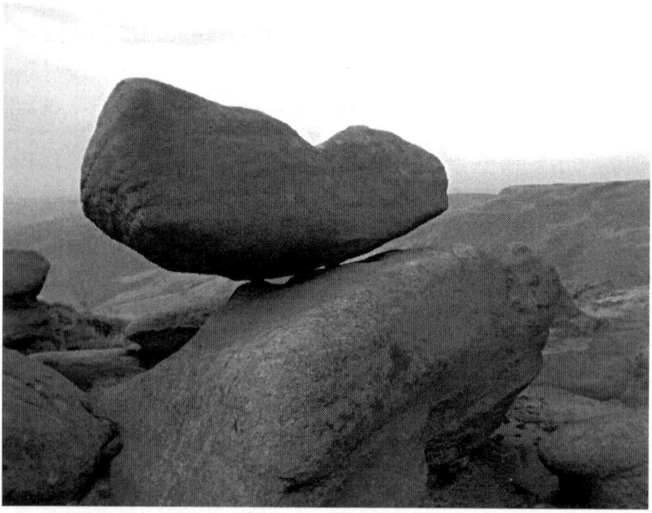

Epilogue

The car pulled up outside the Nags Head pub in Edale.

"Looks like a nice day for it," said Catherine's dad, nodding approvingly at the weather. "Wish we were coming with you."

We grabbed the bags out of the car and waved goodbye as Mike and Julie drove back home.

"Ha! Look at that!" I laughed, pointing at the sign on the side of the pub. "It still says 'The official start of the Pennine Wa' after all these years."

With its close proximity to Manchester and its surrounding towns, Edale has been a magnet for walkers for years. Thanks to its rail and road links, visiting the Peak District is an easy thing to do, and 8.8m people do so every year. A staggering amount compared to a residential population of 37,905.

Many of them come to walk. Some to do long distance paths like the Pennine Way, but far more come to complete day walks in the area. Over twenty times more people use the Pennine Way for day walks, than for long distance walks.

We were back in Edale to do just that. Not for us – just yet anyway – a return visit to Kirk Yetholm, but a simple hike taking in the trail for several miles before heading off down Doctor's Gate to the town of Glossop.

We were up north visiting family, waving our

toddler at his doting grandparents for a week in October to make up for the fact that we'd be staying in London for Christmas. And with ample childcare at our disposal, we'd taken the opportunity to head out to the hills. Whilst we stood outside the Nags Head, our son could be found splashing merrily in the swimming pool with my mum and sister.

For the pair of us it was a chance to relax and unwind; to not think about the stresses and worries of the world. To not think – too much – about the fact that I'd just resigned from my job with nothing else lined up, that we needed a bigger house, or anything else like that. Just to be carefree for a few hours. To take a deep breath and load up the lungs with some of that beautiful clean air.

"I don't remember any of this," I commented as we left Edale through a wall lined track next to a stream.

"Don't you?" replied Catherine, with a hint of surprise in her voice.

"Nope. Not at all," I added, shaking my head to emphasise my lack of remembrance.

That some of our Pennine Way journey would not be remembered was, to be fair, inevitable. It is 267 miles long after all. Still, it was vaguely disappointing not to even remember what the first mile or so actually looked like.

I was on better ground though soon after as we headed up Jacob's Ladder; the height providing a fine view back at Edale and the valley, beautifully lit by the autumn sun. Ah yes, this was coming back to me now.

Up on Kinder, something had changed though.

"It's all green!" Catherine said with surprise, looking at the mass of green shoots that were growing out of the peat bog.

You don't generally expect to return to a fell some years later and find it looking completely different. In fact you rather take for granted that it's pretty unlikely to have changed at all. Hills don't generally change much.

But Kinder had, and rather noticeably too thanks to some recent conservation work. The National Trust, it turned out, had started a massive project to restore the ground. Drainage gullies would be blocked up and the bogs replanted with cotton grass. We were seeing the very early results of that work, which the National Trust planned would turn Kinder from the moonscape we'd originally walked over, back to the moorland it once was. It was a massive plan; one that would take 50 years to complete. In comparison, the fact that the Nags Head hadn't changed their pub sign in a few years suddenly seemed rather irrelevant.

Lunch time began to approach and seeing a large group of rocks, we headed over to find a sheltered spot where we could munch sandwiches and cake away from the wind.

As we did two other walkers stood up and moved away. Clearly they'd had the same idea as us, but had now finished their refreshment break.

"Best be off then," one of them said to us, as they picked up their bags. "See you in Kirk Yetholm!"

And with that, they headed off into the sun. Two

more walkers heading for the Scottish border, with rucksacks on their back, ready to enjoy – or perhaps endure – everything the Pennine Way could throw at them.

Our story had ended. Theirs had just begun.

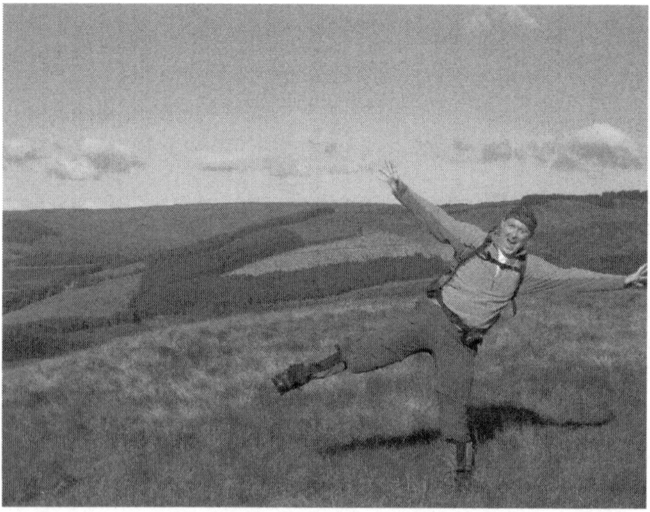

About The Author

Andrew Bowden was born and raised in Hyde, Greater Manchester and spent much of his early years being dragged around Etherow Country Park a few miles from his parents' house.

After abandoning hiking in his teenage years in favour of spending far too much time in front of computer games, he returned to the hills after falling in love with a section of the Pennine Way.

Since rediscovering his hiking boots, he has walked a fair number of long distance trails, including the Coast to Coast, Pennine Way, West Highland Way and the Cumbria Way.

He writes about walking on his website, Rambling Man, at *ramblingman.org.uk*, and can also be found on Twitter at *twitter.com/andrewbowden*

Andrew lives in London with his partner Catherine and son, Sam.

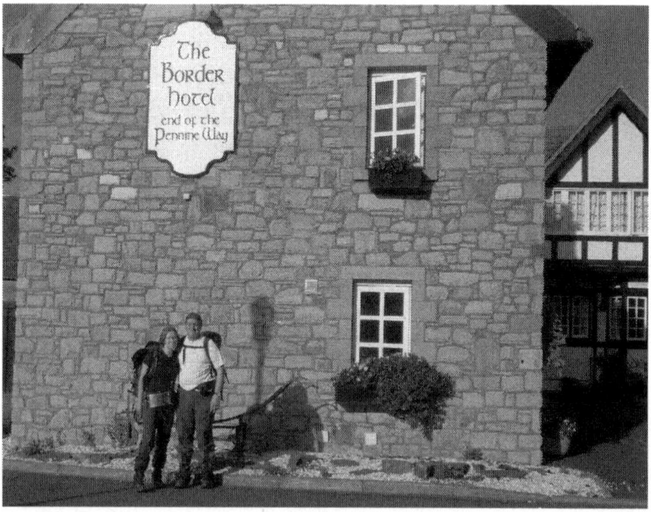
The Border hotel
end of the Pennine Way

Planning your own Pennine Way walk

So you're thinking of walking the Pennine Way, eh? Well good for you. It's certainly an experience and as long as you don't end up up to your waist in bog (and is there anyone who has walked the whole thing, who doesn't end up in bog at least one point?), you'll probably have a good time.

At 267 miles, 467km long it is, however, quite an undertaking to do, especially all in one go, and planning a trip can be hard work so here's some help and advice. A regularly updated version of this guide, complete with links to guide books and online maps can be found on the Rambling Man website at *ramblingman.org.uk*.

What is the walk like?
You may know this already as, after all, the Pennine Way has quite a reputation, but we'll mention it anyway. The simple fact is that the Pennine Way can be a difficult walk.

It passes through a rather remote and quiet part of the country. There's lots of hills, plenty of wild moorland, some long distances and the weather can sometimes be awful. And as for the mud and bog... True, a lot of the worse sections are now paved, however it's one where it's best to be well equipped, especially in the waterproof department.

That said, it is enjoyable and there's no doubt that the sense of achievement when you do it is enormous, however it is probably the toughest and most difficult National Trail that England has to offer. If you're an absolute walking novice, you may wish to try walking a different route first for practise. But then again, you might just want to leap in the deep-end. Just be warned – a walk in the park this is not.

Planning an itinerary

First, let's look at when to walk. From my experience, the Pennine Way is best walked May to September. You can walk it earlier or later, however the weather conditions may not make it a fun experience – even in the summer conditions can be bad underfoot. Walking in late March or early April also runs the risk of snow, especially at the north of the route. Walking during the summer months will give you a more enjoyable walk.

You'll need around three weeks to walk the whole thing. It's not easy to offer set itineraries, as there are several sections, which have lots of accommodation options. As such, I have listed a number of "sections" below – some long and some short. The longer ones are day walks, whilst the shorter sections can be either combined in various ways.

Most – but not – locations listed below have accommodation and a pub. However in some cases accommodation on the trail itself may be limited, and you may need to go off route. More information can be found on the online version of this guide on the Rambling Man website at *ramblingman.org.uk*.

- Edale to Crowden (16 miles, 25¾km)
- Crowden to Standedge (11 miles, 17¾km)
- Standedge to Hebden Bridge (15 miles, 24km)
- Hebden Bridge to Ponden (10¾ miles, 17¼km)
- Ponden to Thornton in Craven (11½ miles, 18½km)
- Thornton in Craven to Gargrave 4½ miles, 7¼km)
- Gargrave to Malham (6½ miles, 10½km)
- Malham to Horton-in-Ribblesdale (14¼ miles, 23km)
- Horton-in-Ribblesdale to Hawes (13¾ miles, 22½km)
- Hawes to Keld (12¼ miles, 19¾km)
- Keld to Tan Hill Inn (4 miles, 6½km)
- Tan Hill Inn to Middleton in Teesdale (16½ miles, 26½km)
- Middleton in Teesdale to Dufton (19 miles, 30½km)
- Dufton to Garrigill (16 miles, 25¾km)
- Garrigill to Alston (4 miles, 6½km)
- Alston to Burnstones/Knarsdale (7 miles, 11km)
- Burnstones/Knarsdale to Greenhead (9 miles, 14½km)
- Greenhead to Once Brewed (6½ miles,

10½km)
- Once Brewed to Bellingham (14½ miles, 23¼km)
- Bellingham to Byrness (14¾ miles, 23¾km)
- Byrness to Kirk Yetholm (via the Cheviot) (27½ miles, 44¼km)
- Byrness to Kirk Yetholm (avoiding the Cheviot) (25 miles, 40¼km)

Breaking the walk up for several trips

If you want to do it all in one go you're going to need about three weeks (and don't forget to include rest days in your planning!) however if you're not able to dedicate that amount of time it is possible to split it up in to several sections.

Public transport connections are better in the southern section of the route meaning you can chunk things up more easily, and the following are some suggestions where good public transport is available – more information on public transport is detailed below.

- Edale to Hebden Bridge (42 miles, 67½km)
- Hebden Bridge to Gargrave (26½ miles, 42½km)
- Gargrave to Horton-in-Ribblesdale (20¼ miles, 32½km)
- Horton-in-Ribblesdale to Dufton (70¾ miles, 114km)
- Dufton to Kirk Yetholm (97¼ miles, 157¼km)

The Bowes Loop Option
After passing the Tan Hill Inn, there are two options for the Pennine Way. One is to keep on the main route, but the other is to follow the Bowes Loop. After several rural sections with few facilities, many will welcome the opportunity to village of Bowes, which has accommodation, pub and a small shop.

- Tan Hill Inn to Bowes (8½ miles, 13½km)
- Bowes to Middleton in Teesdale (12 miles, 19½km)

Options for breaking up Byrness to Kirk Yetholm
The final section of the Pennine Way is the most difficult to sort accommodation for. The final 25 mile (bit more if you go to the Cheviot) stretch goes past no B&Bs and certainly no pubs.

However the Pennine Way walker does have a number of options:

Stay two nights at Kirk Yetholm – most people seem to do this, partly because the local B&Bs are very good at promoting this service. The B&B will pick you up at an arranged location and time and they'll drive you to the village and you can pop to the lovely Border Inn. The next day they'll drive you back and you can continue on to Kirk Yetholm. Note that the pick up points will be a couple of miles off route.

Stay two nights at Byrness – naturally this works in the same way as staying in a Kirk Yetholm

B&B.

Stay somewhere remote – if you're prepared to put up with a long hike off the hill to get to your beds, you could try Barrowburn Farm or Mounthooley Bunkhouse. Both are remote and isolated but well worth visiting.

Stop at a bothy – the National Park operates two shelters. The first is at Yearning Saddle, about eight miles from Byrness. The second is Auchope, about seven miles from Kirk Yetholm. Both are basic shelters so if you plan to stay overnight you'll need food and a sleeping bag. Both are also marked on the Ordnance Survey maps and are on the trail.

Do it all in one day – if you're a glutton for punishment, this is an option. However you'll need to be very fit to manage it.

Note: on some older web pages you may see mention of Uswayford Farm, which was a popular stop-over point and slightly closer to the Pennine Way than Barrowburn. However the B&B closed in 2010 and there is no longer any accommodation or services at Uswayford Farm.

The hostel based itinerary

There was a time when you could do the entire Pennine Way spending pretty much every night under the roof of the YHA, however hostel closures and sell-offs means that's no longer possible. Stepping into the gap have been a number of independent bunk barns, many associated with local pubs, which means most – but not all – of the trail is still covered, with most hostels well spaced for a days walking.

A full guide to hostelling on the Pennine Way can be found on the Rambling Man website at *ramblingman.org.uk*.

Rest Days

If you're planning on doing the Pennine Way all in one go you'll probably want to factor in a rest day or two. The main recommendations are:

Hebden Bridge – a bit early on but this Yorkshire market town has a seriously quirky reputation due to an influx of writers, painters and new age activists in the 1970s and 1980s. There's plenty to explore and enjoy, as well as having regular rail services to Manchester and Leeds

Malham – a popular place for walkers Malham is a lovely place and has a range of walking routes to enjoy.

Horton-in-Ribblesdale – with the three peaks of Ingleborough, Whernside and Pen-y-ghent Horton is a mecca for walkers. The Pennine Way goes over Pen-y-ghent however a rest day can easily be spent exploring the other two peaks or spending some time on the stunning Settle to Carlisle railway line, which passes through the village.

Hawes – this small market town has the Dales Countryside Museum, waterfalls, walking routes and the Wensleydale Creamery.

Bowes – on the Bowes Loop you can spend the day visiting Bowes Castle and other nearby attractions.

Greenhead/Once Brewed – the Pennine Way

runs along part of Hadrian's Wall and highly recommended is to do the short distance between Greenhead and Once Brewed in one day and spend the rest exploring the Roman ruins, museums, and visitor centres.

Finding and booking accommodation

The Pennine Way is well served by accommodation providers of all kinds and you should have no trouble in finding somewhere if booking in advance.

The official Pennine Way website contains a detailed accommodation guide, and can be found at *www.nationaltrail.co.uk/pennine-way/plan*

Due to the limited amount of accommodation in some areas it's advisable to book, however if you don't want to spend three weeks with a rigid itinerary many people report having few problems just turning up and finding a bed. The Pennine Way is also well served with camp-sites and camping barns if you prefer to do things that way.

Just walking the Pennine Way not hardcore enough for you? Well why not do it in style and camp?! The Pennine Way is pretty served by camp-sites, and a number of farms and pubs also offer camping. A full, up to date list of facilities can be found on the Pennine Way website accommodation guide.

The remote countryside for much of the route may appeal to some as perfect for wild camping. However it should be said that conditions on the Pennine Way can often be less than hospitable, with plenty of bogs and mud to be found, especially in wet weather, which means finding a suitable campsite may be difficult. Running water can also be hard to find (unless it's raining!) Under English law you are not legally allowed to wild camp without permission of the landowner.

Getting to/from the Pennine Way

Given the fact that this is a walk between Derbyshire and the Scottish Borders chances are that you're not going to arrive in Edale or Kirk Yetholm by car unless you have some very tolerant friends or family. You'll want to get there by public transport instead.

Useful services are available at or near the following locations:

Edale – on the lovely Hope Valley line roughly half way between Sheffield and Manchester. Trains usually run every two hours, with an hourly service on Saturdays.

Hebden Bridge – several services an hour mostly running between Leeds and Manchester, plus hourly services to Blackpool and York.

Gargrave – a short journey from Leeds, trains also run to Carlisle and Morecambe. Services are sporadic.

Horton-in-Ribblesdale – on the Settle to Carlisle line, trains run through to Carlisle or Leeds roughly every two hours or so.

Dufton – there's no station at Dufton however Appleby on the Settle to Carlisle line is a few miles away. More useful however is 13 miles away at

Penrith, which sits on the West Coast mainline and has regular services to London, Crewe, Carlisle, Glasgow, and Edinburgh. There is very limited public transport from Dufton, which means you'll probably want a taxi.

Byrness – the tiny village is connected to Newcastle by a daily bus, and a daily National Express service, which runs from Wrexham to Perth via Manchester, Leeds, and Newcastle.

Kirk Yetholm – buses to Kelso run at various intervals from just outside the Border Inn. From Kelso there is a two hourly bus service to Berwick-upon-Tweed where railway services regularly run to London, Leeds, York, Newcastle, and Edinburgh amongst other destinations.

Many other locations on the Pennine Way have bus services although they may not be particularly useful to the walker, nor frequent.

Guide Books and Maps

Guidebooks and maps are a must on the Pennine Way. Whilst there are plenty of signs, there are plenty of opportunities to lose your way on the route.

Written by Damian Hall, the latest version of the official *Pennine Way* guidebook was published by Aurum Press in July 2012. Fully updated, it contains information about the trail and (more importantly) Ordnance Survey maps at the 1:25,000 scale. The maps usually show plenty of the area surrounding the route, meaning you don't really need to take any other maps with you.

Whilst not the best ideal for navigation, Wainwright's *Pennine Way Companion* offers AW's own particular take on the walk as well as plenty of history and information. It is a fascinating read. Wainwright's original book has recently been updated by Chris Jesty, along with Wainwright's other pictorial guides to ensure it's up to date.

If you'd like to take maps with you, there are a couple of options. First is the *A-Z Adventure Series* maps. These excellent map books contain Ordnance Survey mapping at the 1:25,000 scale. They're the same size as a folded map so will fit well in your map case, and are a lot easier to change the page for in high wind. The books also contain a full index of places and fells so finding where you want to go is easy. The A-Z have split the Pennine Way over two books. There is one book covering the north, and another for the south.

Alternatively Harveys publish three strip maps, which cover the whole route – Pennine Way South, Pennine Way Central and Pennine Way North. These are Harvey's own mapping, at the 1:40,000 scale.

Alternatively if you'd like Ordnance Survey maps, you will need the following (deep breath):

Landranger (1:50,000): 74, 80, 86, 87, 90, 92, 98, 103, 109, 110

Explorer (1:25,000): OL1, OL2, OL16, OL19, OL21, OL30, OL31, OL42, OL43

Finally, the Pennine Way's fame means that there have been more than a few books written about it.

These include *Walking Home* – poet Simon Armitage's tale of his journey walking home down the Pennine Way (yes, he walks North to South!) Simon acts as a modern day troubadour, trying to arrange a gig every evening and passing round a hat at the end of his performance.

My favourite is *Pennine Walkies*, Mark Wallington's account of walking the trail after deciding his dog, Boogie, needed the exercise. Frequently hilarious, Wallington also has the amazing experience of walking the route with barely any rain, and doesn't fall in any bog at all. Frankly, I suspect he made it all up.

Now out of print, but often available second hand is Barry Pilton's *One Man And His Bog* must surely win the award for best name. Quite why Barry decides to walk the Pennine Way, the reader is never quite sure, but if he hadn't, the world would have one less funny book.

Finally don't forget another out of print book. It's the cartoon based *Laughs Along the Pennine Way*. It's by Pete Bog so it must be good.

Know how to use a map and a compass

Whilst the route is sign posted, there are several parts of the Pennine Way that are difficult to navigate and you'll need to know how to use a map and compass.

There are several online tutorials, easily findable using your favourite search engine. You may also find training courses in your area – many YHA hostels host them for example.

Knowing how to use a map and compass together will really help you and will (hopefully!) stop you getting lost – guide books can only tell you so much in text form.

And finally, and any questions

The Pennine Way is a great challenge to do and I hope the above have given you some useful information to help plan your trip.

So all that is left to do is to get your boots on and get walking! Have fun, and if you have any questions or comments, don't hesitate to ask them over on the Rambling Man website at *ramblingman.org.uk*. You will also find a regularly updated copy of this guide there too.

Discover other books by Andrew Bowden

Find out more about these titles at *ramblingman.org.uk/books*:

- One Coast to Another
- Doing the Dales Way
- The Secret Coast to Coast
- Walking with the Last Prince
- Rambling Man Walks The Ridgeway
- Rambling Man Walks The North Downs Way
- Rambling Man Walks the East Highland Way

Connect with Andrew Bowden

Visit the Rambling Man website:
ramblingman.org.uk

Follow on Twitter:
twitter.com/ramblingmanuk

Find on Facebook:
www.facebook.com/pages/Rambling-Man/253196934720776

Watch on YouTube:
www.youtube.com/user/ramblingmanorguk

Printed in Poland
by Amazon Fulfillment
Poland Sp. z o.o., Wrocław